≋ THE AQUARIL

Cracking the C

with warmest good wishes from

Jane Ridder-Patrick
Consultant Astrologer

Skibo Castle
12th - 13th November 2005

+44 (0) 131 556 2161
jrp@janeridderpatrick.com
www.janeridderpatrick.com

ALSO BY JANE RIDDER-PATRICK

A Handbook of Medical Astrology
Shaping Your Future (Series of 12 titles)
Shaping Your Relationships (Series of 12 titles)

The Zodiac Code series

THE
AQUARIUS
ENIGMA

Cracking the Code

JANE RIDDER-PATRICK

MAINSTREAM
PUBLISHING
EDINBURGH AND LONDON

For Suzann Owings, oustanding psychic, outstanding friend

First published in Great Britain in 2004 by
MAINSTREAM PUBLISHING COMPANY
(EDINBURGH) LTD
7 Albany Street
Edinburgh EH1 3UG

ISBN 1 84018 524 4

A catalogue record for this book is available
from the British Library

Typeset in Allise and Van Dijck

Printed in Great Britain by
Cox & Wyman Ltd

Contents

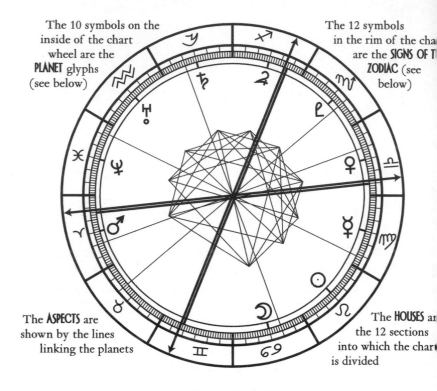

The 10 symbols on the inside of the chart wheel are the **PLANET** glyphs (see below)

The 12 symbols in the rim of the cha[rt] are the **SIGNS OF T[HE] ZODIAC** (see below)

The **ASPECTS** are shown by the lines linking the planets

The **HOUSES** ar[e] the 12 sections into which the chart is divided

A Sample Birth Chart

Sign	Ruler	Sign	Ruler
Aries ♈	Mars ♂	Libra ♎	Venus ♀
Taurus ♉	Venus ♀	Scorpio ♏	Pluto ♇
Gemini ♊	Mercury ☿	Sagittarius ♐	Jupiter ♃
Cancer ♋	Moon ☽	Capricorn ♑	Saturn ♄
Leo ♌	Sun ☉	Aquarius ♒	Uranus ♅
Virgo ♍	Mercury ☿	Pisces ♓	Neptune ♆

ONE

The Truth of Astrology

MOST PEOPLE'S FIRST EXPERIENCE OF ASTROLOGY IS THROUGH newspapers and magazines. This is a mixed blessing for astrology's reputation – writing an astrology column to any degree of accuracy is a tough, many would say impossible, challenge. The astrologer has to try to say something meaningful about conditions that affect every single person belonging to the same sign, over a very short period of time, in a scant handful of words. The miracle is that some talented astrologers do manage to get across a tantalising whiff of the real thing and keep readers coming back for more of what most of us are hungry for – self-knowledge and reassurance about the future. The downside of the popularity of these columns is that many people think that all astrology is a branch of the entertainment industry and is limited to light-hearted fortune-telling. This is far from the truth.

What Astrology Can Offer
Serious astrology is one of the most sophisticated tools available to help us understand ourselves and the world

around us. It gives us a language and a framework to examine and describe – quite literally – *anything* under the Sun, from countries to companies, from money markets to medical matters. Its most common application, however, is in helping people to understand themselves better using their own unique birth charts. Astrology has two main functions. One is to describe the traits and tendencies of whatever it is that is being examined, whether this is a state, a software company or someone's psyche. The other is to give an astonishingly accurate timetable for important changes within that entity. In the chapters that follow, we'll be using astrology to investigate the psychology of the innermost part of your personality, taking a look at what drives, inspires and motivates you.

Astrology uses an ancient system of symbols to describe profound truths about the nature of life on earth, truths that cannot be weighed and measured, but ones we recognise nevertheless, and that touch and move us at a deep level. By linking mythology and mathematics, astrology bridges the gap between our inner lives and our outer experiences, between mind and matter, between poetry and science.

Fate and Free Will

Some people think that astrology is all about foretelling the future, the implication being that everything is predestined and that we have no say in how our lives take shape. None of that is true. We are far from being helpless victims of fate. Everything that happens to us at any given time is the result of past choices. These choices may have been our own, or made by other people. They could even have been made long ago before we, or even our grandparents, were born. It is not always possible to prevent processes that were set in motion in the past from coming to their logical conclusions as events that we then have to deal with. We are, however, all free to decide how to react to whatever is presented to us at every moment of our lives.

Your destiny is linked directly with your personality because the choices you make, consciously or unconsciously, depend largely on your own natural inclinations. It is these inclinations that psychological astrology describes. You can live out every single part of your chart in a constructive or a less constructive way. For instance, if you have Aries strong in your chart, action and initiative will play a major role in your life. It is your choice whether you express yourself aggressively or assertively, heroically or selfishly, and also whether you are the doer or the done-to. Making the right choices is important because every decision has consequences – and what you give out, sooner or later, you get back. If you don't know and understand yourself, you are 'fated' to act according to instinct and how your life experiences have conditioned you. By revealing how you are wired up temperamentally, astrology can highlight alternatives to blind knee-jerk reactions, which often make existing problems worse. This self-knowledge can allow you to make more informed free-will choices, and so help you create a better and more successful future for yourself.

Astrology and Prediction

Astrology cannot predict specific events based on your birth chart. That kind of prediction belongs to clairvoyance and divination. These specialities, when practised by gifted and responsible individuals, can give penetrating insights into events that are likely to happen in the future if matters proceed along their present course.

The real benefit of seeing into the future is that if we

don't like what could happen if we carry on the way we're going, we can take steps either to prevent it or to lessen its impact. Rarely is the future chiselled out in stone. There are many possible futures. What you feed with your attention grows. Using your birth chart, a competent astrologer can map out, for years in advance, major turning points, showing which areas of your life will be affected at these times and the kind of change that will be taking place. This information gives answers to the questions that most clients ask in one way or another: 'Why me, why this and why now?' If you accept responsibility for facing what needs to be done at the appropriate time, and doing it, you can change the course of your life for the better.

Astrology and the Soul

What is sometimes called the soul and its purpose is a mystery much more profound than astrology. Most of us have experienced 'chance' meetings and apparent 'tragedies' which have affected the direction of our entire lives. There is an intelligence at work that is infinitely wiser and more powerful than the will or wishes of our small egocentric personalities. This force, whatever name we give it – Universal Wisdom, the Inner Guide, the Self, a guardian angel – steers us into exactly the right conditions for our souls' growth. Astrology can pinpoint the turning points in the course of your destiny and describe the equipment that you have at your disposal for serving, or resisting, the soul's purpose. That equipment is your personality.

Who Are You?

You are no doubt aware of your many good qualities as well as your rather more resistible ones that you might prefer to keep firmly under wraps. Maybe you have wondered why it is that one part of your personality seems to want to do one thing while another part is stubbornly intent on doing the exact opposite. Have you ever wished that you could crack the code that holds the secrets of what makes you – and significant others – behave in the complex way you do? The good news is that you can, with the help of your astrological birth chart, sometimes known as your horoscope.

Just as surely as your DNA identifies you and distinguishes you from everyone else, as well as encoding your peculiarities and potential, your birth chart reveals the unique 'DNA fingerprinting' of your personality. This may seem a staggering claim, but it is one that those who have experienced serious astrology will endorse, so let's take a closer look at what a birth chart is.

Your Birth Chart

Your birth chart is a simplified diagram of the positions of the planets, as seen from the place of your birth, at the moment you took your first independent breath. Critics have said that astrology is obviously nonsense because birth charts are drawn up as if the Sun and all the planets moved round the Earth.

We know in our minds that the Earth moves round the Sun, but that doesn't stop us seeing the Sun rise in the east in the morning and move across the sky to set in the west in the evening. This is an optical illusion. In the same way, we know (or at least most of us know) that we are not really the centre of the universe, but that doesn't stop us experiencing ourselves as being at the focal point of our own personal worlds. It is impossible to live life in any other way. It is the strength, not weakness, of astrology that it describes from your own unique viewpoint how you, as an individual, experience life.

11

Erecting Your Chart

To draw up a full birth chart you need three pieces of information – the date, time and place of your birth. With your birth date alone you can find the positions of all the planets (except sometimes the Moon) to a good enough degree of accuracy to reveal a great deal of important information about you. If you have the time and place of birth, too, an astrologer can calculate your Ascendant or Rising Sign and the houses of your chart – see below. The Ascendant is a bit like the front door of your personality and describes your general outlook on life. (If you know your Ascendant sign, you might like to read more about its characteristics in the book on that sign in this series.)

The diagram on page 6 shows what a birth chart looks like. Most people find it pretty daunting at first sight but it actually breaks down into only four basic units – the planets, the signs, the aspects and the houses.

The Planets

Below is a simple list of what the planets represent.

PLANET	REPRESENTS YOUR URGE TO
☉ The Sun	express your identity
☽ The Moon	feel nurtured and safe
☿ Mercury	make connections
♀ Venus	attract what you love
♂ Mars	assert your will
♃ Jupiter	find meaning in life
♄ Saturn	achieve your ambitions
♅ Uranus	challenge tradition
♆ Neptune	serve an ideal
♇ Pluto	eliminate, transform and survive

The planets represent the main psychological drives that every single one of us has. The exact way in which we express these drives is not fixed from birth but develops and evolves throughout our lives, both consciously and unconsciously. In this book we will be examining in detail four of these planets – your Sun, Moon, Mercury and Venus. These are the bodies that are right at the heart of our solar system. They correspond, in psychological astrology, to the core of your personality and represent how you express yourself, what motivates you emotionally, how you use your mind and what brings you pleasure.

The Signs
The signs your planets are in show how you tend to express your inner drives. For example, if your Mars is in the action sign of Aries, you will assert yourself pretty directly, pulling no punches. If your Venus is in secretive Scorpio, you will attract, and also be attracted to, emotionally intense relationships. There is a summary of all of the signs on p. 128.

The Aspects
Aspects are important relationships between planets and whether your inner characteristics clash with or complement each other depends largely on whether or not they are in aspect and whether that aspect is an easy or a challenging one. In Chapter Six we'll be looking at some challenging aspects to the Sun.

The Houses
Your birth chart is divided into 12 slices, called houses, each of which is associated with a particular area of life, such as friendships, travel or home life. If, for example, you have your Uranus in the house of career, you are almost

certainly a bit of a maverick at work. If you have your Neptune in the house of partnership, you are likely to idealise your husband, wife or business partner.

The Nature of Time
Your birth chart records a moment in time and space, like a still from a movie – the movie being the apparent movement of the planets round the earth. We all know that time is something that can be measured in precise units, which are always the same, like seconds, months and centuries. But if you stop to reflect for a moment, you'll also recognise that time doesn't always feel the same. Twenty minutes waiting for a bus on a cold, rainy day can seem like a miserable eternity, while the same amount of time spent with someone you love can pass in a flash. As Einstein would say – that's relativity.

There are times in history when something significant seems to be in the air, but even when nothing momentous is happening the quality of time shifts into different 'moods' from moment to moment. Your birth chart is impregnated with the qualities of the time when you were born. For example, people who were born in the mid-to-late 1960s, when society was undergoing major disruptive changes, carry those powerful energies within them and their personalities reflect, in many ways, the turmoil of those troubled and exciting times. Now, as adults, the choices that those individuals make, based on their own inner conflicts and compulsions, will help shape the future of society for better or worse. And so it goes on through the generations.

Seed Meets Soil
There is no such thing as a good or bad chart, nor is any one sign better or worse than another. There are simply 12

different, but equally important, life focuses. It's useful to keep in mind the fact that the chart of each one of us is made up of all the signs of the zodiac. This means that we'll act out, or experience, *every* sign somewhere in our lives. It is true, however, that some individual charts are more challenging than others; but the greater the challenge, the greater the potential for achievement and self-understanding.

In gardening terms, your chart is a bit like the picture on a seed packet. It shows what you could become. If the seeds are of poppies, there's no way you'll get petunias, but external conditions will affect how they grow. With healthy soil, a friendly climate and green-fingered gardeners, the plants have an excellent chance of flourishing. With poor soil, a harsh climate or constant neglect, the seeds will be forced to struggle. This is not always a disadvantage. They can become hardy and adapt, finding new and creative ways of evolving and thriving under more extreme conditions than the plant that was well cared for. It's the same with your chart. The environment you were raised in may have been friendly or hostile to your nature and it will have done much to shape your life until now. Using the insights of astrology to affirm who you are, you can, as an adult, provide your own ideal conditions, become your own best gardener and live out more fully – and successfully – your own highest potential.

TWO

The Symbolism of Aquarius

WE CAN LEARN A GREAT DEAL ABOUT AQUARIUS BY LOOKING AT the symbolism and the myths and legends associated with it. These are time-honoured ways of describing psychological truths. They carry more information than plain facts alone and hint at the deeper meanings and significance of the sign.

The Aquarius glyph of two zigzag parallel lines has been interpreted in many ways over the years. The upper line is said to represent the wisdom of the universe while the lower one is the rational human mind, open to receive it. Aquarians are known both for their detached logic and for their flashes of insight into the bigger picture of life on earth. The lines in parallel also point to the esoteric truth on which astrology itself is based – 'As above, so below' – meaning that heaven and earth mirror each other.

The glyph is sometimes seen as two serpents running along side by side. Serpents have traditionally been linked with wisdom and forbidden knowledge. It was a serpent that tempted Eve to eat the fruit of the Tree of Knowledge. By rebelling against God, Adam and Eve acquired human freedom and also consciousness of themselves as separate individuals. That, however, cost them their place in paradise. This is a familiar theme for Aquarians who, in their quest for Truth and Freedom, often rub the powers-that-be up the wrong way and find themselves shown the door, ending up as exiles and outsiders.

As the wave-like lines of the glyph are the same as the Egyptian hieroglyph for water, and the name Aquarius comes from the Latin word aqua, meaning water, it's hardly surprising that many people think that Aquarius is a water sign. It is, in fact, an air sign. Water was the nearest image the ancients could find to describe the subtle energy that, nowadays, we would think of as being closer to electricity, thought waves or radio signals. This invisible energy is what directs and operates the external world, in the same way that electricity powers computers and washing machines, and the human mind directs wars or mercy missions. Understanding how to harness electricity has revolutionised our everyday lives; understanding that we are all brothers and sisters under the skin can revolutionise the workings of society. Both of these, technology and democracy, are fundamental Aquarian themes. The waves of the glyph don't show water at rest, but rippling forward, in the same way that Aquarian progressive ideas want to move humanity on from selfishness and ignorance towards a new age of enlightenment.

Aquarius the Waterbearer

The Aquarius symbol is the waterbearer, a man with an urn, usually shown in the kneeling position. Just as the Sun radiates energy, in the form of heat and light, the waterbearer generously pours out the contents of his jug for the benefit of all of humanity, without exception. What is in the pitcher, though, is not ordinary water, but offerings of living truth from the vast ocean of what has been called Universal Mind, the sum total of all knowledge in the universe. As an Aquarian, you are often the bringer of fresh ideas and insights to enlighten and improve the world, and can be hurt and frustrated when others just can't see what is so blindingly obvious to you.

The Rulers of Aquarius

Aquarius is ruled by, or associated with, two very different planets – Uranus and Saturn. The modern ruler of Aquarius is Uranus, planet of revolution and progress, which was discovered in 1781. Its discovery shattered the traditional view of the planetary system and coincided with the Industrial Revolution and the great social upheavals in Europe, including the French Revolution, whose aims were greater democracy. With its axis almost at right angles to the Earth, and its moons that revolve backwards, Uranus certainly doesn't conform to the norm – just like most Aquarians.

The traditional ruler of Aquarius is Saturn, the guardian of time, tradition and toil. Many Aquarians seem to favour one ruler over the other. Saturnian Aquarians are dedicated to improving society. They appreciate established values, but promote better controls and new laws and social guidelines, while recognising that some restrictions are necessary for freedom to flourish – and that one person's freedom ends where it infringes another's. The more purely Uranian Aquarians can prefer rebellion, revolution and even anarchy. You are at your best when you combine the patience, practicality and responsibility of Saturn with the insights, experimentation and humanitarianism of Uranus.

Aquarius in Myth and Legend

The myth of Prometheus is closely linked with Aquarius. His name means 'the one who foresees' because of his ability to see clearly into the future. One story tells that he created the human race out of clay and water, which the goddess of wisdom, Athene, breathed life into. Prometheus always showed great goodwill towards humans and it was only his energetic intervention that saved the day when Zeus, the chief god, threatened to exterminate them because they were becoming too clever and powerful. Prometheus even stole fire from the gods to give to the human race. Harnessing the power of fire helped create civilisation, not only because it gave warmth and light in the darkness, bringing longer days and protection from the hardships of nature, but also because it allowed technology to develop. This eased the burden of work and offered society more control over its own destiny. Fire also represents the light of consciousness, and the ability to see ahead to where we are going – all important Aquarian themes.

However, Prometheus was punished by Zeus for bestowing this gift on humankind. He was chained naked to a rock, and each day a vulture tore out his liver, which then grew back overnight. (In the end, he was pardoned and promoted to heaven.) In the life of most Aquarians there comes a time when, because of your desire to improve the lot of others, to enlighten and to speak the truth, you feel 'punished' or treated as an alien because of your ideas, which are so far ahead of their time. Like Prometheus, too, many Aquarians who were rebels and troublemakers in their youth are promoted to the establishment in later life.

The Season of Aquarius

The weather during Aquarius's month can be bleak and miserable, yet the earth is quickening as spring approaches.

This is when the Chinese celebrate New Year. In the middle of all of the fixed signs is an ancient fire festival, marking an important turning point of the year. Aquarius's fire festival, Imbolc, which falls half-way between the winter solstice and the spring equinox, is probably the least well-known. Its Christian equivalent is Candlemas and in the USA it is marked by Groundhog Day. At this time, in most of the northern hemisphere, the days have lengthened sufficiently not to have to depend on candles, or artificial light. Symbolically, this suggests the growth of spiritual light, or enlightenment, and the promise of better days to come.

THREE

The Heart of the Sun

O THE GLYPH FOR THE SUN IS A PERFECT CIRCLE WITH A DOT in the centre and symbolises our dual nature — earthly and eternal. The circle stands for the boundary of the personality, which distinguishes and separates each individual from every other individual, for it is our differences from other people that make us unique, not our similarities. The dot in the centre indicates the mysterious 'divine spark' within us and the potential for becoming conscious of who we truly are, where we have come from and what we may become.

The Meaning of the Sun

Each of your planets represents a different strand of your personality. The Sun is often reckoned to be the most important factor of your whole birth chart. It describes your sense of identity, and the sign that the Sun was in when you were born, your Sun sign, along with its house position and any aspects to other planets, shows how you express and develop that identity.

Your Role in Life

Each of the signs is associated with certain roles that can be played in an infinite number of ways. Take one of the roles of Aries, which is the warrior. A warrior can cover anything from Attila the Hun, who devastated vast stretches of Europe with his deliberate violence, to an eco-warrior, battling to save the environment. The role, warrior, is the same; the motivation and actions are totally different. You can live out every part of your personality in four main ways – as creator, destroyer, onlooker or victim. How you act depends on who you choose to be from the endless variations possible from the symbolism of each of your planets, but most particularly your Sun. And you do have a choice; not all Geminis are irresponsible space cadets nor is every Scorpio a sex-crazed sadist. This book aims to paint a picture of what some of your choices might be and show what choices, conscious or unconscious, some well-known people of your sign have made.

Your upbringing will have helped shape what you believe about yourself and out of those beliefs comes, automatically, behaviour to match. For example, if you believe you are a victim, you will behave like one and the world will happily oblige by victimising you. If you see yourself as a carer, life will present you with plenty to care for – and often to care about, too. If you identify yourself as an adventurer, you'll spot opportunities at every corner. If you're a winner, then you'll tend to succeed. Shift the way that you see yourself and your whole world shifts, too.

Your Vocation

Your Sun describes your major life focus. This is not always a career. As the poet Milton said: 'They also serve who only stand and wait.' It is impossible to tell from your Sun sign exactly what your calling is – there are people of all signs occupied in practically every area of life. What is important is not so much *what* you do, but the way that you do it and it is this – how you express yourself – that your Sun describes. If you spend most of your time working at an occupation or living in a situation where you can't give expression to the qualities of your Sun, or which forces you to go against the grain of your Sun's natural inclinations, then you're likely to live a life of quiet, or possibly even noisy, desperation.

On Whose Authority

Your personality, which your birth chart maps, is like a sensitive instrument that will resonate only to certain frequencies – those that are similar to its own. Your Sun shows the kind of authority that will strike a chord with you, either positively or negatively, because it is in harmony with yours. It can show how you relate to people in authority, especially your father. (It is the Moon that usually shows the relationship with your mother and home.) In adult life it can throw light onto the types of bosses you are likely to come across, and also how you could react to them. It is a major part of the maturing process to take responsibility for expressing your own authority wisely. When you do so, many of your problems with external authorities diminish or even disappear.

In a woman's chart the Sun can also describe the kind of husband she chooses. This is partly because, traditionally, a husband had legal authority over his wife. It is also because, especially in the early years of a marriage, many women choose to pour their energies into homemaking and supporting their husbands' work in the world, rather than their own, and so his career becomes her career. As an

Aquarian, you may find that your father, boss or husband shows either the positive or negative traits of Aquarius or, as is usually the case, a mixture of both – unselfish, friendly and principled or aloof, contrary and emotionally clumsy.

Born on the Cusp

If you were born near the beginning or end of Aquarius, you may know that your birthday falls on the cusp, or meeting point, of two signs. The Sun, however, can only be in one sign or the other. You can find out for sure which sign your Sun is in by checking the tables on pp.98–9.

FOUR

The Drama of Being an Aquarius

EACH SIGN IS ASSOCIATED WITH A CLUSTER OF ROLES THAT HAVE their own core drama or storyline. Being born is a bit like arriving in the middle of an ongoing play and slipping into a certain part. How we play our characters is powerfully shaped in early life by having to respond to the input of the other actors around us – the people that make up our families and communities. As the play of our lives unfolds, we usually become aware that there are themes which tend to repeat themselves. We may ask ourselves questions like 'Why do I always end up with all the work / caught up in fights / with partners who mistreat me / in dead-end jobs / successful but unhappy . . .?' or whatever. Interestingly, I've found that people are less likely to question the wonderful things that happen to them again and again.

The good news is that once we recognise the way we have been playing our roles, we can then use our free-will choice to do some creative re-scripting, using the same character in more constructive scenarios. Even better news is that if we change, the other people in our dramas have got to make some alterations, too. If you refuse to respond to the same old cues in the customary ways, they are going to have to get creative, too.

A core role of Aquarius is the scientist. A scientist searches for the truths, or universal principles, that explain how the world, and all that is in it, operates. As a scientist, your first step is to stand back from the action and observe carefully whatever has attracted your curiosity, whether this is the flight path of a bumblebee or the behaviour patterns of individuals. You then come up with a theory as a possible explanation of what is going on.

A true scientist needs to be impartial and to have the intellectual courage to seek, and speak, only the truth, even if this is contrary to common consensus. George Bernard Shaw said that all great truths begin as blasphemies. If you get emotionally attached to your theories, and can't let them go when evidence shows them to be flawed, you're on the slippery slope to bigotry. It's said in science that new theories are rarely accepted until the old scientists die off. Similarly, some Aquarians can stay married to their fixed ideas until death them do part.

It takes ingenious experiments to test whether your theory corresponds to the data you've collected. You may have an idea that your sister is bad-tempered because she is working too hard. You watch her reactions when she has more work, and then less work, to see if that affects her moods. If she's just as peppery in both situations, it's back to the drawing board to find a new theory. If she's sweet and smiling without the pressure, and explosive with it, you're on firmer ground. Your theory seems to work and you can test it out on others.

Some scientists are content to find the truth for its own sake, but most want to use their discoveries to improve the world. By understanding the laws of life, both social reforms and technologies can be developed. These bring great benefits by relieving people of unnecessary work, and make for greater equality and social justice – but science has to be used responsibly. Upsetting the balance of nature, or society, always has a cost – and it's sometimes a heavy one. The film *Jurassic Park* showed how well-meaning scientists played God by creating monsters that then got out of control and turned destructive. The same thing happened in the French Revolution, where attempts to implement the ideas of Liberty, Fraternity and Equality led to a brutal bloodbath. In science, high ideals need to be balanced with practical wisdom. Unfortunately, many Aquarians are highly intelligent, but lack common sense. You are at your finest when you combine the gifts of your ruling planets – the down-to-earth realism and responsibility of Saturn with the insightfulness and love of experimentation and progress that come with Uranus.

Other Aquarian roles are the rebel, revolutionary, anarchist, humanitarian, reformer, educator, technologist, eccentric, alien and outsider, all of which challenge the status quo and try to put something better, or just different, in its place.

How you choose to see your role will determine your behaviour. The following chapter describes some typical Aquarius behaviour. Remember, though, that there is no such thing as a person who is all Aquarius and nothing but Aquarius. You are much more complicated than that and other parts of your chart will modify, or may even seem to contradict, the single, but central, strand of your personality which is your Sun sign. These other sides of your nature will add colour and contrast and may restrict or reinforce your basic Aquarius identity. They won't, however, cancel out the challenges you face as an Aquarian.

FIVE

The Aquarian Temperament

THE SAYING 'A FRIEND IN NEED IS A FRIEND INDEED' COULD HAVE been coined with Aquarians in mind. You're almost always ready to drop whatever you're doing to help out a friend – but hate asking favours for yourself. Once your friend, always your friend – unless you've been badly let down and then you'll withdraw – more sad and puzzled than angry. You might never see acquaintances from one decade to the next, but then, suddenly, take a notion to track them down and turn up on their doorstep, all smiles, and carry on where you left off, as if you had seen them only a day or so before. It may often be a case of out of sight, out of mind, but certainly not out of your heart or address book.

The Lone Ranger
You'd love to connect with just about everyone on the planet, briefly, as you're curious about other people's activities and ideas, especially if they are different from your own. Sociable and gregarious, you love to feel part of the group. Cooperating with kindred spirits for a common purpose is one of your favourite activities. But you're also a

bit of a loner and need solitude and your own space, too. You can have many friends but few intimates and even then you're unlikely to allow them entry to your innermost private space.

Unselfish Service

A selfless impulse to help others is your most powerful driving force and you'll often sacrifice your own interests for the greater good of all. As you tend to think and speak in terms of 'we' rather than 'me', you've a horror of being selfish, and can torture yourself with a whole litany of high-principled ideals about how you should or shouldn't behave, which can lead you to ignoring your own needs and feelings. Psychologically, that's not healthy. The kindness and consideration that you show towards others needs to be applied to yourself, too. It's much better to indulge yourself occasionally, instead of always putting others first and allowing unconscious resentment to build up.

Nobody Special

With your belief in equality, you much prefer to be one of the crowd, and may even keep quiet about your own distinctions and achievements in case they mark you out as special or privileged, something that makes you feel acutely uncomfortable. Yet, no matter how noble your ideals, you too have an ego that needs to be recognised. All of the signs benefit from an infusion of the qualities of the opposite sign, which in your case is Leo. Leos are upfront and open about wanting love and admiration – and their desire to rule the roost. Suppressing these perfectly normal human drives can make you, quite unconsciously, start to elbow out those who don't agree with your ideas and plans, and sabotage your ability to lighten up and enjoy fun.

Equality for All

As you think on a global scale, you're deeply concerned about the welfare of humanity as a whole, rather than focusing exclusively on your own backyard. To you, all humans are kith and kin despite differences of race, colour, nation, creed or class. You have no time for elitism, snobbery or social distinctions, and injustice towards any group makes you to want to stand up and act on their behalf. You believe that everyone should have equal rights, and not just the privileged few. Your ideal, like Aquarian Abraham Lincoln, in his ringing words from the Gettysburg Address, is 'government of the people, by the people, for the people'. Wherever you see or hear the word 'rights' being demanded by or for some group, you can be sure there is Aquarian energy around. When you support a campaign, you'll throw yourself into it with determination, no matter what the personal cost. Lincoln, despite stiff opposition, successfully fought to abolish slavery and declare legal equality between blacks and whites, and was assassinated for his troubles.

Honest Injun

You are highly principled and, believing in fairness and integrity at all times, you'll rarely tell a deliberate lie. You hate hypocrisy and double-dealing but can be subtly dishonest yourself, sometimes using your detachment to fool the unwary. One Aquarian businessman sat through a meeting of industry chiefs where price-fixing was being arranged, silent, listening, and making no objections. Next day, when the boss of the biggest firm rang to set the plans in motion, the Aquarian replied, in total honesty, that he'd agreed to nothing, and the whole crooked deal collapsed.

The Grand Plan

With your dedication to truth, freedom and experimentation, as well as your urge to improve the system, more than likely you have plans for a better world – and your own ideas about how this should come about. It's said that there is nothing more powerful than an idea whose time has come, and it's these timely and world-shifting ideas that grip your attention and move you to action.

You'll happily work to overthrow the existing system if it interferes with your vision of progress, but you have an authoritarian streak yourself. Some Aquarians see nothing wrong with forcing others to conform to their plans and with demanding that all people be equal and free – provided it's done their way. It's easy to mount the moral high ground because your intentions are usually genuinely good, unselfish and honourable, and you can be mortified, or outraged, when this hypocrisy is pointed out to you.

Experimental Genius

You love to experiment with new ways of doing things. Why follow tradition when there might be a new and better approach? This makes you a natural inventor, rebel and trend-setter. Some Aquarians are so far ahead of their time that they seem to straddle, or even cross, the notoriously thin line between genius and madness – though the world's definition of madness is often itself insane, and simply means 'doesn't fit in'. Thomas Edison was thrown out of school for being retarded, then went on to patent inventions that have radically changed our daily lives, like the light bulb, the gramophone and moving pictures. As George Bernard Shaw said: 'The reasonable man adapts himself to the world: the unreasonable one persists in trying to adapt the world to himself. Therefore all progress depends on the unreasonable man.' Like an Aquarian, in other words.

Quite Contrary

'Ah – but . . .' is a favourite Aquarian expression, as your mind clicks reflexly into a contradiction. You probably enjoy defying public opinion, and shocking the staid with your eccentric behaviour and doing exactly the opposite of what 'normal' people would do. 'Hell,' said W.C. Fields, 'I never vote *for* anybody, I always vote *against*.' Even disguised in a bland grey suit or twin-set and pearls, your flashes of adolescent rebellion against anyone in authority will sooner or later give you away. Your mind can be inconsistent, too. You can be quite disparaging about, say, alternative medicine, then go on to talk about something twice as weird, like alien abductions, as if this were a commonly accepted fact of life.

Watching and Weighing

To feel safe, watery types – those with Cancer, Scorpio or Pisces strong in their charts – need the reassurance of ongoing emotional rapport, so they often mistake your silences and detachment for chilling disapproval. That's rarely true. More often, you're merely standing back, all the better to assess what's going on, and reserving your judgement. You don't take things at face value and, in the final analysis, will make your own decisions about people and situations. Once you have accepted a person, you'll stay loyal and no amount of gossip will change your mind. One wise Aquarian I know always refuses to be drawn into character assassination, saying simply, 'That person is my friend.'

The Search for Truth

When it comes to truth and freedom – as you understand them – you'll make no compromise, regardless of who approves or who doesn't. You'll stand by your ideas, even if you end up isolated – a lone and lonely voice crying in the wilderness. Neither force nor persuasion will move you, as you are no moral coward and are willing to pay the price for championing your convictions – which is often being misunderstood and alienated from the very people you are trying to help. Some Aquarians, however, cling stubbornly and perversely to their own pride and prejudices. There is nothing more effective in cutting you off from the truth than the belief that you know it already. As Aquarius is a fixed sign, flexibility is not your strong point. You'll refuse to be pushed, pulled or pressured into making any changes, in your opinions or anything else, but when you do, you can alter course drastically and then be equally resolute about your new direction.

Feeling Phobic

The emotional detachment that serves you – and the world – so well, by allowing you to see the panoramic view, is also responsible for your biggest headache and challenge. This is your difficulty with expressing, or even tolerating, feelings. While you'll endlessly scrutinise the motivations of other people to help them change, you are tight-jawed averse to examining yourself too closely. If anyone tries to penetrate your deep, dark and complex emotional nature, you'll react as if you've been violated. Panic, repulsion, impatience, embarrassment or anger are your reactions to emotional turbulence, passion and drama, which you condemn as signs of weakness or selfishness and treat as if they were something unpleasant you would scrape off your shoe.

You're on safe ground with anything that can be solved with the mind, but you have little real understanding of, or empathy with, the murk and mire of the instinctual side of human nature – especially your own. It's been said of Aquarians that you love humanity but don't much like people.

Loose Wiring

Being so emotionally detached, you can treat people more like chess pieces than creatures of flesh, blood and feelings. You mean well, but at times can be toe-curlingly insensitive to the subtleties of human interactions. Sometimes you just appear to lack the layer of circuitry that's responsible for emotional intelligence and interpersonal skills. Many Aquarians are drawn to psychology because they love observing, and making maps and models of human behaviour, but they are often oblivious to the fact that the map is not the territory and can be unsympathetic and clueless when it comes to meeting human nature in the raw. One leading light in the field of counselling told me, with distaste, that he thought that clients who vented or wallowed in their feelings should be made to pay double fees. Another Aquarian friend can't bear to watch Shakespeare's great drama of jealousy, *Othello*, as the hero seems to her to be such a stupid fellow who can't be bothered to listen. You just don't see the point of feelings so you'll repress your own, sometimes ruthlessly, which means that you are frequently, though unintentionally, emotionally dishonest.

Checking the Data

The way you *think* you are feeling can at times be wildly uncoupled from the reality of what you actually *are* feeling.

One Aquarian, Margaret, rushed to her sister on a mercy mission. When, because of her tightly folded arms, the scowl on her face, the frequent surreptitious glances at her watch, plus an atmosphere of resentment radiating from her that could be cut with a knife, her sister accused her of not wanting to be there, Margaret was genuinely shocked and denied it vehemently. She decided, though, to check the data. Looking at herself in the mirror she realised, with amazement, that her sister was right and slowly the penny dropped that she had come out of duty and would much rather be at home getting on with her own life. Now, when she remembers, Margaret still checks in the mirror for clues about what she's feeling. You might like to, too, or have a friend give you feedback, when your body language is screaming louder than words.

Aquarius at Work

You've little personal ambition and the motivations that drive others – like money, power and fame – have, for you, no truly compelling attraction. So, without a push from the outside, you can end up as a drifter and wasting your talents, which are often considerable. Many Aquarians find themselves in their jobs by following the path of least resistance. It's hard for you to sit down and plan what you want to do and then commit yourself to one course of action. So circumstances often dictate your path and prospects, and if you don't get on, you can act the misunderstood genius, blaming the unappreciative world for not being ready for your talents. Left to your own devices, you'd probably cheerfully stay out to lunch, thinking about life, rather than living it. It's not that you are lazy or work-shy, although there is part of you that would secretly like to be kept by the state – or by anybody else who is willing to slave from nine to five to subsidise your theorising. You are at your happiest, though, when your strong social conscience is put to good use and are more than capable of pulling your weight and putting your back into anything that you believe is worthwhile, and for the good of all.

Systems Analysis

Positions where you have fresh stimuli, problems to solve, people to study and the freedom to get on with your work in your own way are right up your street. You've the mind of a chess player and can stand back from the action, making a coolly detached assessment of what's going on in the big picture, without getting bogged down or side-tracked. Analysing systems is your speciality. You are ace at drawing up maps of key areas, spotting snags and bottlenecks, weighing facts and coming up with fresh insights and experiments and suggestions for overhauls and upgrading. You're brilliant at taking a badly run business, or department, and using your logic and finely tuned intuition to devise elegant solutions for radical improvements. You usually don't bother to exert yourself to win approval and would rather just get on with what needs doing and, in the process, sometimes manage to rub others up the wrong way.

Earning a Crust

Because you prefer to cooperate rather than compete, teamwork suits you well, as does work which affects society as a whole, such as social work, education, psychology, law, human rights and politics. You could also be attracted to mathematics, computing or innovative technologies. You're not particularly interested in money for its own sake. It's more a means of buying your precious freedom. Aquarians who are rich have usually inherited it or come by it accidentally, either through their inventions, or by just happening to be in a job they enjoy that makes them plenty of money. You are capable of pouring every penny you have – and possibly more – into any project that captures your imagination with only a glancing thought for tomorrow and, unless your back is to the wall, can be quite indifferent to financial ups and downs.

Aquarius and Health

Aquarius rules the lower legs, especially the calves and ankles, as well as the circulation; it is the contraction of the large muscles at the back of the lower legs that pumps the blood back to the heart. All of the rhythmic and electrical activity in the body is also associated with Aquarius. This includes the nervous system, the light receptors of the eyes and the processes that maintain the correct balance of chemicals inside each cell. Esoterically Aquarius is said to rule the aura, the body's source of vitality.

Varicose veins, thromboses, poor circulation and, in later years, heart disorders can affect some Aquarians. Much of this can be avoided by plenty of fresh air, sleep and exercise. Walking and cycling are especially recommended, while jobs involving long hours of standing are best avoided. Being so lost in your thoughts and preoccupied with helping others, you are often out of touch with your own physical and emotional needs. Like an absent-minded professor, you can completely ignore your body's prompting to eat and sleep at the proper times. Although your constitution is generally strong, it's easy to push yourself to exhaustion without noticing, and constant neglect could eventually take its toll.

Nervous Tension

While it would be hard to guess it from your cool exterior, you can be quite a worrier. Your highly active brain and nervous system can go into overdrive, making it hard to rest and relax. You can be sensitive to fluctuations of temperature and atmosphere and develop allergies to things you don't want to deal with. Clumsiness and lack of coordination, as well as nervous tics, palpitations and insomnia and, occasionally, more serious or obscure nervous system disorders are all Aquarian maladies. Psychologically, some of these can be linked to hardening of the attitudes but, with sensible care and attention, prolonged good health should be well within your reach.

Aquarius Relating

Relationships are, for many Aquarians, a minefield. Altruism and friendship you understand; in these, you are gifted. Love is another matter altogether because this is intimate, personal and exclusive, themes which make you nervous, so you'll you tend to shy away from getting emotionally entangled. Even with your wide network of friends, you're everybody's chum but nobody's exclusive best buddy. Because you like almost everyone and feel you should belong to them all equally, some Aquarians resist seeing any one person as special, for that would make them more equal than others. This can leave partners feeling like just one of a cast of thousands – and very, very angry. Close relationships with Aquarians like these are not for the sensitive or the egotistical.

You tend to view life from afar, like a spectator watching a fascinating game. Love and relating, however, are not spectator sports and if you don't learn to participate, even when you are with another Aquarian, you're likely to encounter a few difficulties. Because you can see emotions as unwanted and unacceptable demands, you are rarely prepared to invest much into a relationship at the feeling level, and may be completely unaware of how dependent you yourself can be.

Roses with Thorns

Unless there is a substantial water presence in your chart, romantically you may be a little clumsy and obtuse, as the nuances and niceties of relating can be a bit of a mystery to you. Your insistence on telling the truth when a tactful white lie would be more appropriate can bruise a partner's feelings, and your insistence on fairness, at the wrong moment, can be downright infuriating. Often you can't understand the need for flowers, flattery and affection and the tiny romantic gestures that oil the machinery of happy and successful relationships. Yes, it's irrational, but making efforts here, with good grace, could pay enormous dividends.

Friendship and Freedom

You don't like too much togetherness or possessiveness – and you certainly don't appreciate your need for freedom being curtailed, or your work being interrupted, by the restricting burdens of domesticity. It's ideal when your partner is also your best friend, and someone who won't make heavy emotional demands on you. The road to your heart is through your mind, and you'd often prefer a nice, safe, platonic companionship, with an optional add-on sexual component. While you can thoroughly enjoy sex, your attitude towards it can be rather detached and you'll be horrified if any playmate reads more into it than what you clearly stated. And those who become clingy or cloyingly possessive with you can expect a severe case of frostbite.

Loyal and True

Once committed, you make a kind, considerate, devoted and emotionally loyal partner. You have your own moral code which may, or may not, include physical fidelity. You usually don't care much for illicit relationships, as lies are not your style, and are far too much trouble to remember anyway. You are rarely a fiery or passionate lover, much more considerate, affectionate and often experimental. If you have slept with someone once and didn't enjoy it, you may give him or her a second chance, just to work out exactly what it was that made you so incompatible.

Clean Breaks

You have a lot of pride and won't show your feelings, no matter how much you are hurting, and if, after giving it your best shot, a relationship doesn't work out, you will turn cold and cut off, wasting no time on jealousy or regrets. The Aries boyfriend of an Aquarian had psyched himself up to tell her their romance was over. She took the wind out of his sails by coolly thanking him for his consideration in letting her know. 'Is that it?' he demanded, adrenalin surging, ready for a fight. 'That's it,' she replied, mentally shifting gear to single status and recalling that she'd worked out from previous experience that it takes two weeks to clear a partner's energy out of the system. No doubt she also added the classic Aquarian parting shot: 'Let's be friends. Keep in touch.'

SIX

Aspects of the Sun

PLANETS, JUST LIKE PEOPLE, CAN HAVE IMPORTANT RELATIONSHIPS
with each other. These relationships are called aspects.
Aspects to your Sun from any other planet can influence
your personality markedly. The most powerful effects come
with those from the slower-moving planets – Saturn,
Uranus, Neptune or Pluto. Sometimes they can alter your
ideas about yourself and your behaviour patterns so much
that you may not feel at all typical of your sign in certain
areas of your life.

Check if your birth date and year appear in the various
sections below to find out if one or more of these planets
was aspecting the Sun when you were born. Only the so-
called challenging aspects have been included. These are
formed when the planets are together, opposite or at right
angles to each other in the sky.

Unfortunately, because space is restricted, other aspects
have been left out, although they have similar effects to
those described below and, for the same reason, a few dates
will inevitably have been missed out, too. (You can find out
for sure whether or not your Sun is aspected at my website

www.janeridderpatrick.com.) If your Sun has no aspects to Saturn, Uranus, Neptune or Pluto, you're more likely to be a typical Aquarian.

Some well-known Aquarians with challenging aspects to their Suns appear below. You can find more in the birthday section at the end of the book.

Sun in Aquarius in Aspect with Saturn

If you were born between 1932 and 1934, 1962 and 1964 or 1991 and 1994, whether or not your birthday is listed below, you are likely to feel the influence of Saturn on your Sun.

20–30 January in: 1932–3, 1941, 1947, 1953–4, 1962, 1970, 1976, 1983 and 1991–2

31 January–9 February: 1934, 1941, 1948, 1955, 1963, 1971, 1977, 1984 and 1992–3

10–19 February in: 1935, 1938, 1948, 1955–6, 1964, 1972, 1985 and 1993–4

Abraham Lincoln	Wolfgang Amadeus Mozart	Mary Quant
Kirsty Wark	Oprah Winfrey	Virginia Woolf

From childhood you've probably had to carry a heavy burden of responsibility, and your self-esteem may have taken some hard knocks for not living up to other people's expectations. If you still believe, as an adult, that you are a victim of officials who are out to censor and frustrate you, you can become stubbornly uncooperative. You are then quite capable of acting so awkwardly that those in command are practically forced to reprimand you, reinforcing your belief that all authority stinks.

You have a powerful drive to prove yourself as a reformer, progressive thinker or leader of the avant-garde, and to have your achievements recognised. This may accompany a secret dread that you're really not good enough and will be found out and humiliated. Fear, of either success or failure, could make you shy away from doing what it takes to become an achiever. While you dislike standing out from the crowd by being privileged and special, you long to nevertheless, and have both a desire for the approval of the powers-that-be, and an instinctive urge to rebel against them. The real issue, however, is not to overthrow authorities, or to conform to get their approval, it is to tackle the judge inside your head that drips out discouraging messages. When you face squarely your own inner bogey of self-doubt and depression, you can build up a solid sense of who you are, and what you can become. By biting the bullet and submitting to Saturn's demands – patience, hard work and discipline – you can, like Abraham Lincoln and Oprah Winfrey, work towards your real goal of freeing yourself and others from the oppression of the past and shouldering some responsible role in society.

Sun in Aquarius in Aspect with Uranus

20–30 January in: 1935–8, 1954–8 and 1974–7
31 January–9 February in: 1938–41, 1958–62, and 1977–9
10–19 February in: 1940–4, 1960–2, and 1978–82

Lewis Carroll	Colette	Charles Dickens
Germaine Greer	Jackson Pollock	Vanessa Redgrave

No way are you going to toe anyone else's line. Social injustice and being expected to do things just because that's the way they have always been done are, to you, like red rags to a bull. You probably have quite a knack of creating controversies. Germaine Greer caused shockwaves by stating that no woman who hadn't tasted her own menstrual blood could consider herself 'liberated'. At best, you have a crystal-clear view of what is outdated or unfair in a system and have advanced ideas of how to bring about improvements. Charles Dickens, through his novels brought the world's attentionn to gross social injustices. At worst, you can be a bit of an oddball or just downright contrary. You also have the courage to stick to your convictions. The actress Vanessa Redgrave says that she chooses her roles carefully so that when she retires they will have covered the full range of oppression in recent history. She has never backed down from her political opinions even when it has alienated the influential and lost her career opportunities.

Flouting convention and shocking people can give you a kick but it can be lonely out there at the cutting edge as rebel, innovator or inventor. You tend to be ahead of your time and often out of step with where the common herd finds itself today. Although your ideas sometimes appear completely off the wall or totally outrageous, often, when enough time has passed, what was so innovative and strange when you first came up with it becomes absorbed into mainstream thinking and is then considered just plain common sense. Being tied down rarely appeals to you and though you can be loyal and steadfast – in your own way – you need plenty of breathing space in relationships.

Sun in Aquarius in Aspect with Neptune

20–30 January in: 1955–62
31 January–9 February in: 1960–7
10–19 February in: 1964–71

| Jennifer Aniston | Thomas Edison | W.C. Fields |
| Yoko Ono | Franklin D. Roosevelt | Virginia Woolf |

Neptune heightens your sensitivity to other people's fantasies and suffering. You long to cater for the first and either alleviate, or retreat from, the other. You're a natural for working in the worlds of beauty, film, advertising, arts or fashion – or in the caring professions. Things are never quite what they seem when Neptune, planet of spirituality, as well as illusion, is involved. It's hard to pin you down, either physically or emotionally. Others may see you as a saviour, or an icon, or a helpless victim in need of rescuing. You may be all of these things – or none. It's probably hard for you, too, to know who you are. You may often experience a sense of vague anxiety, disappointment, or even unworthiness, when your perfect vision of how the world should be clashes with how it actually is. It's easy to become addicted, and allergic, to anything that gives relief from harsh reality, so take care how you choose your bliss. Music, poetry or even daydreams are preferable to chocolate biscuits, illness – or alcohol, W.C. Fields' favourite escape route. He was one of the most prolific drinkers of his time.

On the positive side, your intuition is strong, and when you pay attention to it and put its promptings into practice, you can work wonders. As Thomas Edison said, 'To invent, you just need a good imagination and a pile of junk.' There may be a strongly spiritual, or devotional, side to your nature and this is where this combination shows up at its best. When you find a cause that you passionately believe in and throw yourself into it heart and soul, you have found your way home.

Sun in Aquarius in Aspect with Pluto

If you were born between 1938 and 1956, whether or not your birthday appears below, you are likely to feel the effect of Pluto on your Sun.

20–30 January in: 1937–47 and 1983–8
31 January–9 February in: 1944–53 and 1987–92
10–19 February in: 1950–9 and 1990–6

Alfred Adler	Margaux Hemingway	John McEnroe
Sharon Tate	John Travolta	Edith Wharton

Pluto means power, and this will come into your life in one form or another – as wealth, sex, death, dogmatic ideologies or emotionally charged situations. Your career could involve one or more of these areas. American author Edith Wharton often portrayed her characters as tragic victims of cruel social conventions. Either you will be the one wielding power, so that nobody gets to push you around – or you could find yourself at times feeling under threat, with your back against the wall. Your relationship with your father, or bosses, may involve intense power struggles, sometimes made worse by your sense of vulnerability, or your unwillingness to compromise. Alfred Adler said that every attempt to dominate others stems from an inferiority complex, a term he introduced to psychology.

You're unlikely to tolerate corruption, hypocrisy or bullying, all of which you can spot instantly, and will rarely rest until you've exposed, and dealt with, the culprits. It's not easy for you to trust life and you can be secretive for self-protection. But you are a survivor and often operate best when living on the edge. As an Aquarian, looking at the darker side of life and human selfishness, especially your own, repels you, but with this aspect you can't escape it. You may have a sense that there is something unacceptable about you. Your challenge is not to look away, but to learn to use power wisely, refusing to be either a victim or a tyrant. You can then become a powerful agent for positive transformation in your work or community. At some time you are likely to make a radical shift in your career, or sense of identity. This is something to be celebrated, not feared.

SEVEN

Meeting Your Moon

D THE GLYPH FOR THE MOON IS THE SEMI-CIRCLE OR CRESCENT. It is a symbol for the receptiveness of the soul and is associated with feminine energies and the ebb and flow of the rhythms of life. In some traditions it represents the gateway to paradise and the realms of bliss.

The Sun and Moon are the two complementary poles of your personality, like yang and yin, masculine and feminine, active and reflective, career and home, father and mother. The Moon comes into its own as a guide at night, the time of sleeping consciousness. It also has a powerful effect on the waters of the earth. Likewise, the Moon in your birth chart describes what you respond to instinctively and feel 'in your waters', often just below the level of consciousness. It is your private radar system, sending you messages via your body responses and feelings, telling you whether a situation seems safe or scary, nice or nasty. Feelings provide vital information about circumstances in and around you. Ignore them at your peril; that will lead you into emotional, and sometimes even physical, danger. Eating disorders tend to be associated with being out of touch with, or neglecting, the instincts and the body, both of which the Moon describes.

Extraordinary though it might seem to those who are emotionally tuned in, some people have great difficulty in knowing what they are feeling. One simple way is to pay attention to your body. Notice any sensations that attract your attention. Those are linked to your feelings. Now get a sense of whether they are pleasant or unpleasant, then try to put a more exact name to what those feelings might be. Is it sadness, happiness, fear? What is it that they are trying to tell you? Your Moon hints at what will strongly activate your feelings. Learning to trust and decode this information will help make the world seem – and be – a safer place.

The Moon represents your drive to nurture and protect yourself and others. Its sign, house and aspects describe how you respond and adapt emotionally to situations and what feeds you, in every sense of the word. It gives information about your home and home life and how you experienced your mother, family and childhood, as well as describing your comfort zone of what feels familiar – the words 'family' and 'familiar' come from the same source. It shows, too, what makes you feel secure and what could comfort you when you're feeling anxious. Your Moon describes what moves and motivates you powerfully at the deepest instinctual level and indicates what is truly the 'matter' in – or with – your life.

Knowing children's Moon signs can help parents and teachers better understand their insecurities and respect their emotional make-up and needs, and so prevent unnecessary hurt, or even harm, to sensitive young lives. It's all too easy to expect that our children and parents should have the same emotional wiring as we do, but that's rarely how life works. Finding our parents' Moon signs can be a real revelation. It can often help us understand where they are coming from, what they need and why they react to us in the way they do. Many of my clients have been able to find the understanding and compassion to forgive their parents when they realised that they were doing their very best with the emotional resources available to them.

In relationships it is important that your Moon's requirements are met to a good enough extent. For example, if you have your Moon in Sagittarius you must have adventure, freedom and the opportunity to express your beliefs. If being with your partner constantly violates these basic needs, you will never feel secure and loved and the relationship could, in the long term, undermine you. However, if your Moon feels too comfortable, you will never change and grow. The art is to get a good working balance between support and challenge.

A man's Moon sign can show some of the qualities he will unconsciously select in a wife or partner. Some of the others are shown in his Venus sign. Many women can seem much more like their Moon signs than their Sun signs, especially if they are involved in mothering a family and being a support system for their husbands or partners. It is only at the mid-life crisis that many women start to identify more with the qualities of their own Suns rather than living that out through their partners' ambitions. Similarly, men tend to live out the characteristics of their Moon signs through their wives and partners until mid-life, often quite cut off from their own feelings and emotional responses. If a man doesn't seem at all like his Moon sign, then check out the women in his life. There's a good chance that his wife, mother or daughter will show these qualities.

Your Moon can be in any sign, including the same one as your Sun. Each sign belongs to one of the four elements: Fire, Earth, Air or Water. The element of your Moon can give you a general idea of how you respond to new situations and what you need to feel safe and comforted. We all become anxious if our Moon's needs are not being recognised and attended to. We then, automatically, go into our personal little rituals for making ourselves feel better. Whenever you are feeling distressed, especially when you are way out of your comfort zone in an unfamiliar situation, do something to feed and soothe your Moon. You're almost certain to calm down quickly.

Fire Moons

If you have a fire Moon in Aries, Leo or Sagittarius, your first response to any situation is to investigate in your imagination the possibilities for drama, excitement and self-expression. Feeling trapped by dreary routine in an ordinary humdrum life crushes you completely. Knowing that you are carrying out a special mission feeds your soul. To you, all the world's a stage and a voyage of discovery. Unless you are at the centre of the action playing some meaningful role, anxiety and depression can set in. To feel secure, you have to have an appropriate outlet for expressing your spontaneity, honourable instincts and passionate need to be of unique significance. The acknowledgement, appreciation and feedback of people around you are essential, or you don't feel real. Not to be seen and appreciated, or to be overlooked, can feel like a threat to your very existence.

Earth Moons

If you have an earth Moon in Taurus, Virgo or Capricorn, you'll respond to new situations cautiously and practically. Rapidly changing circumstances where you feel swept along and out of control are hard for you to cope with. You need time for impressions to sink in. Sometimes it is only much later, after an event has taken place, that you become sure what you felt about it. Your security lies in slowing down, following familiar routines and rituals, even if they are a bit obsessive, and focusing on something, preferably material – possibly the body itself or nature – which is comforting because it is still there. Indulging the senses in some way often helps too, through food, sex or body care. So does taking charge of the practicalities of the immediate situation, even if this is only mixing the drinks or passing out clipboards. To feel secure, you need continuity and a sense that you have your hand on the rudder of your own life. Think of the rather irreverent joke about the man seeming to cross himself in a crisis, all the while actually touching his most valued possessions to check that they are still intact – spectacles, testicles, wallet and watch. That must have been thought up by someone with the Moon in an earth sign.

Air Moons

When your Moon is in an air sign – Gemini, Libra or Aquarius – you feel most secure when you can stand back from situations and observe them from a distance. Too much intimacy chokes you and you'll tend to escape it by going into your head to the safety of ideas and analysis. Even in close relationships you need your mental, and preferably physical, space. You often have to think, talk or write about what you are feeling before you are sure what your feelings are. By putting them 'out there' so that you can examine them clearly, you can claim them as your own. Unfairness and unethical behaviour can upset you badly and make you feel uneasy until you have done something about it or responded in some way. It can be easy with an air Moon to be unaware of, or to ignore, your own feelings because you are more responsive to ideas, people and situations outside of yourself that may seem to have little connection with you. This is not a good idea, as it cuts you off from the needs of your body as well as your own emotional intelligence. Making opportunities to talk, play with and exchange ideas and information can reduce the stress levels if anxiety strikes.

Water Moons

Finally, if your Moon is in a water sign – Cancer, Scorpio or Pisces – you are ultra-sensitive to atmospheres, and you can experience other people's pain or distress as if they were your own. You tend to take everything personally and, even if the situation has nothing at all to do with you, feel responsible for making it better. Your worst nightmare is to feel no emotional response coming back from other people. That activates your deep-seated terror of abandonment, which can make you feel that you don't exist and is, quite literally, what you fear even more than death. If you feel insecure, you may be tempted to resort to emotional manipulation to try to force intimacy with others – not a good idea, as this can lead to the very rejection that you dread. You are at your most secure when the emotional climate is positive and you have trusted, supportive folk around who will winkle you out of hiding if you become too reclusive. With a water Moon, it is vital to learn to value your own feelings and to take them seriously – and to have a safe, private place you can retreat to when you feel emotionally fragile. As you never forget anything which has made a feeling impression on you, sometimes your reactions are triggered by unconscious memories of things long past, rather than what is taking place in the present. When you learn to interpret them correctly, your feelings are your finest ally and will serve you well.

Finding Your Moon Sign

If you don't yet know your Moon sign, before looking it up, you could have some fun reading through the descriptions that follow and seeing if you can guess which one it is. To find your Moon sign, check your year and date of birth in the tables on pp.100–113. For a greater in-depth understanding of your Moon sign, you might like to read about its characteristics in the book in this series about that sign.

At the beginning of each section are the names of some well-known Aquarians with that particular Moon sign. You can find more about them in Chapter Ten.

Sun in Aquarius with Moon in Aries

Plácido Domingo   Isabelle Eberhardt   Gennifer Flowers
Barry Humphries   Henry Morton Stanley Virginia Woolf

You thrive on challenge, usually the tougher the better. In 1869, journalist Henry Morton Stanley received the curt instruction from his New York newspaper boss, 'Find Livingstone'. Two years and many adventures later, he finally tracked down the missionary in the heart of Africa, greeting him coolly with 'Dr Livingstone, I presume?'.

You are a livewire and a firebrand and, with your strong independent streak, you can't bear being told what to do. It would be surprising if you haven't had some stormy run-ins with those in authority. Boredom, lack of freedom and a peaceful, humdrum life would be intolerable to you, just as it was for Isabelle Eberhardt. A nineteenth-century Swiss aristocrat, she ran away to Algeria, became a Muslim and, disguised as a man, she worked as a dock labourer, did as she pleased and had countless affairs, thumbing her nose at convention. Some whose need for action and daring is stifled can become miserably unhappy and produce skin rashes, depression or migraines, all symptoms of blocked Aries energy. Sadly, Virginia Woolf, author of the ground-breaking feminist classic A *Room of One's Own*, found her own deep depressions (Saturn aspected her Sun, too) and debilitating headaches so intolerable that she turned the aggressive Aries energy against herself, choosing to take her own life.

Your unshakeable belief in your own projects can make you an inspiring leader and a force to be reckoned with. You need to be careful not to be high-handed, as it's not always easy for you to appreciate another's point of view. You are not exactly subtle and can be rather insensitive when it comes to other people's agendas or feelings, but you're the best possible person to have around where there are barricades in need of storming.

Sun in Aquarius with Moon in Taurus

Geena Davis	Germaine Greer	Somerset Maugham
Ronald Reagan	Patricia Routledge	Jackson Pollock

Your practical and common-sense approach to whatever life throws at you makes you a dependable rock for everyone. But you can be every bit as unbudgable as that same rock and may even be a bit of a control freak. Once you've set your course, it's hard for you to shift. Your will is formidable. You will plod away doggedly until you have achieved whatever you have set your heart on, dealing with each obstacle as it appears, until all resistance is worn down. Your determination is rarely self-serving. All of your efforts are directed at improving conditions — especially for peace and prosperity – for the community you serve and, as you see it, for the benefit of the world. Quoting directly from the White House website: 'Overall, the Reagan years saw a restoration of prosperity, and the goal of peace through strength seemed to be within grasp.'

With your sound business instincts, you have what it takes to ground your vision and produce concrete and lasting results. Security for you lies in the simple things in life – owning your own home, good food and sex, enough in the bank – and being in complete control. If events move too fast, and you feel swept off centre, anxiety sets in and insecurity can make you dictatorial. Real security, however, lies in developing a solid sense of your own worth, which cannot be bought or borrowed. It's important to step off the roundabout at regular intervals and recharge your batteries at the slow pace of your own heartbeat. If you feel under stress, spending time outdoors is the answer. An hour or two in the garden building walls or breaking ground, or walking the golf course or hills, would do you the world of good.

Sun in Aquarius with Moon in Gemini

| Prue Leith | John McEnroe | Jack Nicklaus |
| Thomas Paine | Kirsty Wark | Jane Seymour |

Pens and ink, phones and e-mails could have been invented with you in mind. Not being able to communicate, share and comment on your experiences almost continuously is, for you, like oxygen starvation. Incurably curious and sometimes downright nosy, you love to keep up to date with whatever's fresh in your field. At home, more than likely you'll have the radio, television and two computers on at the same time and still manage to sneak a look at the newspapers.

It's hard for you to stick to just one career or, if you do, to remain at the same task or position for too long. You need variety and frequent change to keep your mind fed and whirring with fresh ideas. You'd much prefer to stay a free spirit and never fully grow up. Homemaking and settling down are likely to be the biggest challenges in your life; you may even prefer two places you can call home. You'll love the fun of playing with children but the responsibilities and constant grind of domesticity could feel like a ball and chain if you can't get out to play, too.

Words fascinate you, especially puns, and you love to play games with them. With your needle-sharp wit, you've the ability to bring together incongruous ideas with wackily hilarious results. You can use your clever tongue to talk your way in or out of tricky situations and you do like to have the last word. Like versatile TV presenter Kirsty Wark, you'd make an excellent reporter, political commentator, writer and mimic, as you are quick to pick up the essence of what is going on and pass it on to others with a few telling words, gestures or strokes of the pen.

Sun in Aquarius with Moon in Cancer

Linda Blair	Lord Byron	Christian Dior
Clark Gable	Jacqueline du Pré	Boris Yeltsin

Man or woman, you've a great need to give and receive mothering and unconditional acceptance. Clark Gable called his glamorous wife, Carole Lombard, 'Ma' and she called him 'Pa', although they had no children together.

You feel deeply and are easily moved to tears and,

underneath that cool and detached exterior, you are likely to be more sensitive, reclusive and timid than you care to admit, even to yourself. Being highly intuitive, you pick up on atmospheres instantly and are quick to respond to the needs of others – a great asset if you work with the public, as they in turn tend to respond positively to you. You are terrified of humiliation and rejection and to protect yourself you may become cynical. Lord Byron, who had a club foot, became a Don Juan ladykiller after being hurt to the quick by overhearing a woman say that she could never love a cripple. Rumour has it that his deepest and longest lasting affair was with his own half-sister. It's essential to find some way of expressing or discharging your feelings of resentment quickly, or they can turn inwards and eat away at you as body symptoms.

Mother, or mother country, is important to you but if you were hurt in childhood you can put your emotions on ice, or even cut off completely from your birth family. Your greatest challenge is to learn to work with your feelings, neither ignoring them away nor allowing them to engulf and overwhelm you. They are allies, not enemies, especially when you learn to respect and decode them. It's when you find ways of championing and cherishing society's most vulnerable members that your finest qualities blossom.

Sun in Aquarius with Moon in Leo

James Joyce	Gypsy Rose Lee	Jack Lemmon
François Rabelais	Oliver Reed	Alice Walker

Dramatic, warm-hearted and flamboyant, you've a charismatic personality that's larger than life. Confidence and self-promotion usually come easily to you, though you can seesaw between wanting to be the focal point of the universe and just one of the crowd. More than likely you're a natural group leader, with formidable organising skills. Being overlooked, or appearing insignificant, can leave you feeling anxious. So it's vital that you find some place in your life where it's appropriate for you to be the centre of attention, where you can stand in the spotlight radiating honour and integrity. It's equally important, too, that you use your glorious pizzazz to spearhead reforms, be experimental or challenge the established way of doing things – especially if it improves the lot of others. Even as a young child, the author and civil-rights activist Alice Walker loved to stand up in church and give speeches.

You've a tendency to show off when you're feeling insecure, and when everything isn't going your way you could even throw a temper tantrum or two. You've a knack of getting your own way and, with your open-handed generosity and happy self-confidence, any opposition to your plans usually melts away like snow in sunshine. In relationships, you need to be adored and, as you much prefer to be boss, this can lead to tussles over who rules the roost and gets to sit on the throne. You gravitate towards all that is of the finest and most glorious in life and in human nature, and won't tolerate the shoddy or the second-rate, and why should you? As having fun feeds you, make sure you don't miss out on any of it.

Sun in Aquarius with Moon in Virgo

| Eva Braun | W.C. Fields | Virginia Johnson |
| John Travolta | James Watt | Sophie, Countess of Wessex |

With your analytical skills and love of experimentation, you can be a gifted problem-solver and deal-broker. Work that you see as useful, or leading to some clearly defined end result, brings you great satisfaction. James Watt developed the steam engine that paved the way for the Industrial Revolution. You'll go to endless trouble to get the specifics right. Virginia Johnson, with her husband William Masters, spent eleven years studying, in meticulous detail, the psychology and physiology of sexual intercourse in volunteer couples under laboratory conditions.

Sloppiness, especially in thinking, can drive you to distraction. With your ability to spot a flaw, in a system or a sentence, at a hundred paces, you've a highly critical mind, and often a tongue to match. You like to get things right and can be nitpickingly fault-finding with yourself, and with others, if you believe a job has been botched up. While you'll enjoy ticking off achievements on those never-ending to-do lists that whirr round in your head, it's best not to let them run your life or get bogged down in detail. Being rushed, or having your schedules interrupted, irritates and flusters you. But you can have a refreshingly pragmatic approach to life. As W.C. Fields said, 'If at first you don't succeed, try, try and try again. Then give up. There's no use being a damned fool about it.'

A familiar domestic schedule is a major source of comfort but when you feel insecure, you'll tend to work harder and go into obsessive little rituals, often around body care or exercise. Simplicity suits you well, so cutting down to essentials and dejunking your life could be a perfect tonic from time to time.

Sun in Aquarius with Moon in Libra

Bertolt Brecht	Ruth Rendell	Jerry Springer
Muriel Spark	Maria von Trapp	Norman Wisdom

You'll do almost anything to avoid any powerful emotions that threaten to engulf you. On the other hand – that's a phrase you'll use frequently – you are excellent at dealing with other people's psychological or social problems at a distance – a bit like an umpire watching a tennis match. Standing well back from the firing line, you can take a detached view of all sides in disputes.

The Aquarian need for social improvement and Libra's drive towards peace and justice make you a front-line candidate for politics or strategic planning. You like to appear as Mr or Ms Nice and hate to be thought of as unfair, selfish or unlikable. Anybody who thinks you're a pushover, though, is in for a few surprises. Behind that gentle, courteous manner is the mind of a chess player and the wiliness of a seasoned diplomat. You have your opponents sized up and have worked out where they are coming from and what they want. You'll bide your time and then act, to your own advantage, when the opportune moment arrives. If there is an atmosphere of disharmony around, or you sense that you have offended someone, you won't feel comfortable till you've patched matters up. But too nice is as bad as too nasty; if things become too cosy and agreeable, you'll deliberately stir up controversy just to see what happens, then have the pleasure of smoothing down ruffled feathers. Jerry Springer always ends his battleground TV shows with a honeyed little homily. You can be altruistic to the point of naivety and neglect your own needs, then wonder why you get irritable. Being fair to yourself isn't selfish – it's just plain common sense.

Sun in Aquarius with Moon in Scorpio

Helen Gurley Brown	Alex Comfort	James Dean
Michael Hutchence	Edith Wharton	Robbie Williams

With your friendly good nature, you may seem transparent and open, yet it's hard to get close to you, as you tend to be secretive about the depth and intensity of your feelings. You guard your privacy fiercely and prefer people to know about you only what you choose. Many with this combination radiate an aura of power or sexuality. It would be surprising if life hadn't brought you into contact with sex, death, secrets, wealth or political power, one way or another, in early life, and these themes could continue to fascinate, or follow you, into adult life. Alex Comfort wrote the celebrated bestseller *The Joy of Sex*, and Helen Gurley Brown, editor-in-chief of *Cosmopolitan* magazine, renowned for its raunchy content, caused shock waves in the 1960s with her *Sex and the Single Girl*.

You are capable of deeply loyal and long-lasting relationships, but if your trust is ever betrayed the hurt goes deep and you may forgive but never, ever, forget.

You've a gut instinct about what is really going on beneath the polite façade of human interactions and won't feel comfortable until you've tracked down and eliminated anything that is shady, corrupt or just plain 'off' in your own home patch. You are acutely sensitive to people whose survival is threatened, as you can identify with them, and are drawn to help them. Your deep reserve of emotional power comes to your aid when your back is to the wall. In fact, you often feel most alive under extreme conditions and could go out of your way to attract them. You may surprise even yourself with how resourceful a survivor you are, and how threat can bring out the best – or the worst – in you.

Sun in Aquarius with Moon in Sagittarius

Jennifer Aniston	Robert Burns	Charles Dickens
David Jason	Charles Lindbergh	Oprah Winfrey

Sunny Sagittarius gives you faith in life, no matter what it throws at you, as well as a compelling wanderlust that can be physical, mental or restlessly romantic. Fidelity may not come easily to you because of your hunger for exploring foreign parts. Scotland's national poet, Robert Burns, enjoyed broadening his outlook through rubbing shoulders with sailors and smugglers, and his frequent, and passionate, falling in and out of love earned him a Don Juan reputation and regular public chastisements from the pulpit of the Kirk. You love to follow your dreams and trust your luck, no matter how big the risk. Charles Lindbergh achieved world fame as the first person to fly solo and non-stop from New York to Paris in 1932, while David Jason's characters, like Del Boy, are cheeky chancers, running rings round authority.

Generous to a fault, you probably love splashing the cash around and rarely count the cost. You live on the assumption that supply is unlimited and, anyway, worrying about life's limitations, to your mind, is somebody else's business. Housekeeping is rarely your forte cither, and you need a partner who can share your enthusiasms and who will give you plenty of freedom. Behind the mask of the entertainer, you could plunge into depression if unwanted responsibilities pile up, or you are tied down tightly and not allowed out to play.

To find the meaning of life is your Holy Grail and you're

almost certainly a natural philosopher. Being both a perpetual student and a life-long teacher – sometimes preacher – giving advice comes as easily as breathing. When you've found a new nugget of wisdom, you love to pass it on. Like Oprah Winfrey, you can be an inspired coach, encouraging others to reach for the stars. The fields of teaching, publishing and broadcasting could be highly profitable for you.

Sun in Aquarius with Moon in Capricorn

Charles Darwin	Mia Farrow	Betty Friedan
Abraham Lincoln	Michael Bentine	Mary Quant

Hard work, and sometimes hardship, is as familiar to you as breathing. Charles Darwin's theory of evolution by natural selection sent shock waves through the Church establishment. The first edition of his book, *The Origin of Species*, sold out in a single day. Despite suffering constant ill health and panic attacks, he laboured at his task of writing it, slowly and painfully, until it was completed. His spirit lives on in you. Totally committed to whatever you see as your duty, you will stick at any task doggedly, overcoming every obstacle until success is yours. This self-discipline means you are well-fitted for positions of responsibility – unless you're one of the few who give up and succumb to gloom and despair.

Doing the right thing matters to you, and this can sometimes lead to overworking or staying, inappropriately, in unsatisfying jobs or relationships. As you mature, though, you're likely to become adept at rejecting the crushing burden of other people's expectations. You're prone to hiding emotional needs for fear of disapproval and can be judgmental about those who don't follow your preferred rules of conduct. In childhood, material or emotional support may have been in short supply, while the family kept up appearances for fear of what the neighbours might think. There's a bonus in this. You are capable of looking after yourself, and others, in practically any situation. While, at heart, you're a rebel or reformer, you still honour tradition and old-fashioned virtues. Becoming a respected leader and elder in your community would give you great satisfaction. You've an ironic sense of humour that can cover up a deep layer of sadness. A measure of solitude, and even melancholy, can be therapeutic for you, so don't try to banish it from your life entirely.

Sun in Aquarius with Moon in Aquarius

Queen Beatrix	Elizabeth Blackwell	Colette
Havelock Ellis	Jeanne Moreau	Princess Stephanie

Fitting into a role where you are expected to conform to traditional standards isn't easy for you. Queen Beatrix of the Netherlands has dispensed with much crusty royal formality and is happy to cycle through the streets of Amsterdam like any commoner. Controversial Princess Stephanie of Monaco is even more democratic. She is reported to have three children by two of the palace bodyguards.

Your antennae are set to register injustice, inequality and outworn and (to your mind) senseless conventions, and you'll often feel compelled to slice through, or ignore, any pointless red tape and break new ground. Elizabeth Blackwell successfully fought entrenched attitudes and prejudice to become the first woman doctor in America in

1849. More recently, in 2001, Jeanne Moreau became the first woman ever to be elected to the prestigious French Académie des Beaux-Arts.

You prefer loyal friendships to cosy intimacy. If anybody tries to get too close, either physically or emotionally, you'll start to withdraw. Your home, or lifestyle, is likely to be unusual in some way and this suits you better than a tight-knit, 'normal' nuclear family. Even if you have lived in the same house all your life, you may feel as though you are just camping temporarily, waiting, slightly on edge, for the call to move on. This can stop you putting down emotional roots anywhere and may even lead to relationship tensions with those who need more intimacy. Deep down, you feel the whole world is your family and for contentment you need to find some way of opening and widening your family home or circle to let in the world. Time on your own, as well as with friends, is essential to recharge your batteries.

Sun in Aquarius with Moon in Pisces

Eartha Kitt	Toni Morrison	Paul Newman
Lisa Marie Presley	Claire Rayner	Ken Wilber

Logical and aloof Aquarius linked with dreamy, reclusive and dependent Pisces can be an uncomfortable, or a highly creative, mix. Some are intellectually offended by anything that smacks of the irrational or mystical, yet it will impact on your life somewhere. The finest psychic I know obstinately resisted acknowledging and developing her gift until she was forced to accept how much it helped others. With a heart that aches for the unfortunate, you empathise instinctively with other people's pain, and you feel for those that society overlooks or rejects. Being involved in political campaigning for the underprivileged, or in voluntary work, feeds your need to heal, and to be healed yourself in the process. Paul Newman contributes all of the profits of his highly successful food company to a charity formed after he lost a son to drug addiction.

You can pick up atmospheres instantly, noticing especially if anyone is suffering or expecting something from you. You'll then feel guilty and uncomfortable until you have supplied whatever it is you sense they need. Because of your fear of abandonment, as a child you would have learned to read emotional atmospheres, and how to cater for the emotional needs of others, especially your mother, in order to have your own needs met indirectly. Public figures with Pisces Moons can tap in to, and provide, the magic their audience longs for and so become much-loved icons. Frequent escapes from everyday reality are essential for your well-being, preferably not via alcohol or food, as this can get out of hand. Being so sensitive, choose carefully whom you have around you. Especially dangerous for you is negativity, because you're wide open to psychic contamination. The positive side of this is that you are equally open to the enchantment of poetry, romance and beauty.

EIGHT

Mercury — It's All in the Mind

THE GLYPHS FOR THE PLANETS ARE MADE UP OF THREE SYMBOLS: the circle, the semi-circle and the cross. Mercury is the only planet, apart from Pluto, whose glyph is made up of all three of these symbols. At the bottom there is the cross, representing the material world; at the top is the semi-circle of the crescent Moon, symbolising the personal soul; and in the middle, linking these two, is the circle of eternity, expressed through the individual. In mythology, Mercury was the only god who had access to all three worlds – the underworld, the middle world of earth and the higher world of the gods. Mercury in your chart represents your ability, through your thoughts and words, to make connections between the inner world of your mind and emotions, the outer world of other people and events, and the higher world of intuition. Your Mercury sign can give you a great deal of information about the way your mind works and about your interests, communication skills and your preferred learning style.

It can be frustrating when we just can't get through to some people and it's easy to dismiss them as being either completely thick or deliberately obstructive. Chances are they are neither. It may be that you're simply not talking each other's languages. Knowing your own and other people's communication styles can lead to major breakthroughs in relationships.

Information about children's natural learning patterns can help us teach them more effectively. It's impossible to learn properly if the material isn't presented in a way that resonates with the way your mind works. You just can't 'hear' it, pick it up or grasp it. Wires then get crossed and the data simply isn't processed. Many children are seriously disadvantaged if learning materials and environments don't speak to them. You may even have been a child like that yourself. If so, you could easily have been left with the false impression that you are a poor learner just because you couldn't get a handle on the lessons being taught. Identifying your own learning style can be like finding the hidden key to the treasure room of knowledge.

The signs of the zodiac are divided into four groups by element:

> The fire signs: Aries, Leo and Sagittarius
> The earth signs: Taurus, Virgo and Capricorn
> The air signs: Gemini, Libra and Aquarius
> The water signs: Cancer, Scorpio and Pisces

Your Mercury will therefore belong to one of the four elements, depending on which sign it is in. Your Mercury can only be in one of three signs – the same sign as your Sun, the one before or the one after. This means that each sign has one learning style that is never natural to it. For Aquarians, this is the fire style.

Mercury in each of the elements has a distinctive way of

operating. I've given the following names to the learning and communicating styles of Mercury through the elements. Mercury in fire – active imaginative; Mercury in earth – practical; Mercury in air – logical; and Mercury in water – impressionable.

Mercury in Fire: Active Imaginative
Your mind is wide open to the excitement of fresh ideas. It responds to action and to the creative possibilities of new situations. Drama, games and storytelling are excellent ways for you to learn. You love to have fun and play with ideas. Any material to be learned has to have some significance for you personally, or add to your self-esteem, otherwise you rapidly lose interest. You learn by acting out the new information, either physically or in your imagination. The most efficient way of succeeding in any goal is to make first a mental picture of your having achieved it. This is called mental rehearsal and is used by many top sportsmen and women as a technique to help improve their performance. You do this spontaneously, as your imagination is your greatest mental asset. You can run through future scenarios in your mind's eye and see, instantly, where a particular piece of information or situation could lead and spot possibilities that other people couldn't even begin to dream of. You are brilliant at coming up with flashes of inspiration for creative breakthroughs and crisis management.

Mercury in Earth: Practical
Endless presentations of feelings, theories and possibilities can make your eyes glaze over and your brain ache to shut down. What really turns you on is trying out these theories and possibilities to see if they work in practice. If they don't, you'll tend to classify them 'of no further interest'.

Emotionally charged information is at best a puzzling non-starter and at worst an irritating turn-off. Practical demonstrations, tried and tested facts and working models fascinate you. Hands-on learning, where you can see how a process functions from start to finish, especially if it leads to some useful material end-product, is right up your street. It's important to allow yourself plenty of time when you are learning, writing or thinking out what to say, otherwise you can feel rushed and out of control, never pleasant sensations for earth signs. Your special skill is in coming up with effective solutions to practical problems and in formulating long-range plans that bring concrete, measurable results.

Mercury in Air: Logical

You love learning about, and playing with, ideas, theories and principles. Often you do this best by arguing or bouncing ideas off other people, or by writing down your thoughts. Your special gift is in your ability to stand back and work out the patterns of relationship between people or things. You much prefer it when facts are presented to you logically and unemotionally and have very little time for the irrational, uncertainty or for personal opinions. You do, though, tend to have plenty of those kinds of views yourself, only you call them logical conclusions. Whether a fact is useful or not is less important than whether it fits into your mental map of how the world operates. If facts don't fit in, you'll either ignore them, find a way of making them fit, or, occasionally, make a grand leap to a new, upgraded theory. Yours is the mind of the scientist or chess player. You make a brilliant planner because you can be detached enough to take an overview of the entire situation.

Mercury in Water: Impressionable

Your mind is sensitive to atmospheres and emotional undertones and to the context in which information is presented. Plain facts and figures can often leave you cold and even intimidated. You can take things too personally and read between the lines for what you believe is really being said or taught. If you don't feel emotionally safe, you can be cautious about revealing your true thoughts. It may be hard, or even impossible, for you to learn properly in what you sense is a hostile environment. You are excellent at impression management. Like a skilful artist painting a picture, you can influence others to think what you'd like them to by using suggestive gestures or pauses and intonations. People with Mercury in water signs are often seriously disadvantaged by left-brain schooling methods that are too rigidly structured for them. You take in information best through pictures or images, so that you get a 'feel' for the material and can make an emotional bond with it, in the same way you connect with people. In emotionally supportive situations where there is a rapport between you and your instructors, or your learning material, you are able just to drink in and absorb circulating knowledge without conscious effort, sometimes not even being clear about how or why you know certain things.

Finding Your Mercury Sign

If you don't yet know your Mercury sign, you might like to see if you can guess what it is from the descriptions below before checking it out in the tables on pp.114–15.

Sun in Aquarius with Mercury in Capricorn

Lewis Carroll	Charles Dickens	Germaine Greer
Jerome Kern	Claire Rayner	Muriel Spark

Even if some of your ideas are wildly eccentric, or even downright anarchistic, you can translate them into mainstream conventional language. This gives you an excellent chance of being heard and taken seriously. Achieving recognition for something you have said or written would give you immense satisfaction, as you can sometimes be a little nervous about being judged negatively for how you express yourself. This can make you seem rather formal or reserved, and even slightly frosty or disapproving, in the way you communicate. You can be disparaging or judgmental about any ideas you disagree with and, when it suits you, use tradition to back you up.

Realism can sometimes turn to pessimism and occasionally even depression. One of the songs in Jerome Kern's hugely successful musical classic *Show Boat*, called 'Mis'ry's Comin' Round', was cut when it was first produced as it was so tragic. Usually, though, you're intolerant of self-pity and your attitude is to tell yourself, and others, to pull yourself together and just get on with it. With your practical, administrative mind attuned to making long-term arrangements, you've probably had your pension plans drawn up from an early age. In business deals and contracts, you tend to read the small print carefully, as you've the mindset of a corporate lawyer and are good at spotting pitfalls and loopholes in any project you are involved in. At the back of your mind, there's often a master plan for climbing up your chosen ladder of success. With your practical mind, a formal or traditional approach to learning probably suits you and you may even take a responsible, and innovative, attitude towards helping others learn, as Capricorn is the sign of the community elder.

Sun in Aquarius with Mercury in Aquarius

> Virginia Woolf   Thomas Edison   Wolfgang Amadeus Mozart
> Edith Wharton   Oprah Winfrey   Helen Gurley Brown

You have the ability to express your ideas with breathtaking clarity and logic. It's as if, like Mozart and Edison, your flashes of inspiration sometimes come from a higher realm altogether – and perhaps they do. You can be an outstanding lightning conductor and mouthpiece for circulating ideas whose time has come. Sharing these with like-minded people is your idea of mental bliss. Even better is using your insights for some humanitarian cause that will improve society at large and benefit all.

You can take the long, cool and detached view of any situation you come across, business or personal. This means that you can see facts clearly as they are, and how they fit into the big picture, with very little emotional bias. This has advantages and disadvantages. The advantage is the extent and clarity of your panoramic vision; the down side is the difficulty you may have in understanding, or even tolerating, the value and meaning of irrational feelings or enlightened self-interest.

Truth – as you understand it – matters to you and you'll rarely let convention stand in the way. Once an idea has taken root in your mind, you will stand by it loyally. This can give you great tenacity to follow through on your convictions; but if you get the wrong end of the stick, your thought processes could gallop off into the stratosphere and become wildly uncoupled from reality. Your views are frequently unorthodox but you'll express them, often with a chuckle of delight at the feathers you ruffle. What you say, and how you say it, may shock or shake today, but tomorrow could be taken for granted as plain common sense.

Sun in Aquarius with Mercury in Pisces

Alice Cooper	Charles Darwin	Matt Groening
James Joyce	Yoko Ono	John Travolta

You live half in, and half out, of the world of your imagination and may often seem dreamy and absent-minded. You could have an interest in spiritual matters, recognising that we are all one. Pictures, poetry, images and music help you learn best, by allowing the relevant information to sink in to your impressionable mind. Being practically psychic, you are highly responsive to emotional atmospheres and can pick up on thoughts and ideas that are 'in the air'. You can often be the mouthpiece for saying out loud the anarchic rumblings that everybody else is feeling, just below the surface of consciousness. The Archbishop of Canterbury said of Matt Groening's wildly dysfunctional TV family, *The Simpsons*, that it's one of the most subtle pieces of propaganda around in the cause of sense, humility and virtue.

While Mercury in Aquarius is like a lightning conductor, Mercury in Pisces is more like a delicate and finely tuned musical instrument that resonates to the slightest nuance in the environment. You may find it difficult to distinguish clear boundaries between what you and other people are thinking or saying, so your spirits can rise and fall like a barometer, depending on whose company you are in. Children with this combination often need to be taught, gently but firmly, the difference between fact and fiction, as truth can be relative with this Mercury position. You are a wonderful impression manager, gifted at painting word pictures, which can make you an inspired writer or poet – or con artist. You're also quick to notice other people's suffering and longings for life to be better. By acting on these insights, you can make a great contribution to helping others.

NINE

Venus — At Your Pleasure

♀ THE GLYPH FOR VENUS IS MADE UP OF THE CIRCLE OF ETERNITY on top of the cross of matter. Esoterically this represents love, which is a quality of the divine, revealed on earth through personal choice. The saying 'One man's meat is another man's poison' couldn't be more relevant when it comes to what we love. It is a mystery why we find one thing attractive and another unattractive, or even repulsive. Looking at the sign, aspects and house of your Venus can't give any explanation of this mystery, but it can give some clear indications of what it is that you value and find desirable. This can be quite different from what current fashion tells you you should like. For example, many people are strongly turned on by voluptuous bodies but the media constantly shows images of near-anorexics as the desirable ideal. If you ignore what you, personally, find beautiful and try to be, or to love, what at heart leaves you cold, you are setting yourself up for unnecessary pain and dissatisfaction. Being true to your Venus sign, even if other people think you are strange, brings joy and pleasure. It also builds up your self-esteem because it grounds you solidly in your own personal values. This, in turn, makes you much more attractive to others. Not only that, it improves your relationships immeasurably, because you are living authentically and not betraying yourself by trying to prove your worth to others by being something you are not.

Glittering Venus, the brightest planet in the heavens, was named after the goddess of love, war and victory. Earlier names for her were Aphrodite, Innana and Ishtar. She was beautiful, self-willed and self-indulgent but was also skilled in all the arts of civilisation.

Your Venus sign shows what you desire and would like to possess, not only in relationships but also in all aspects of your taste, from clothes and culture to hobbies and hobby-horses. It identifies how and where you can be charming and seductive and skilful at creating your own type of beauty yourself. It also describes your style of attracting partners and the kind of people that turn you on. When your Venus is activated you feel powerful, desirable and wonderfully, wickedly indulged and indulgent. When it is not, even if someone has all the right credentials to make a good match, the relationship will always lack that certain something. If you don't take the chance to express your Venus to a good enough degree somewhere in your life, you miss out woefully on delight and happiness.

Morning Star, Evening Star

Venus appears in the sky either in the morning or in the evening. The ancients launched their attacks when Venus became a morning star, believing that she was then in her warrior-goddess role, releasing aggressive energy for victory in battle. If you're a morning-star person, you're likely to be impulsive, self-willed and idealistic, prepared to hold out until you find the partner who is just right for you.

Relationships and business dealings of morning-star Venus people are said to prosper best whenever Venus in the sky is a morning star. If you are an early bird, you can check this out. At these times Venus can be seen in the eastern sky before the Sun has risen.

The name for Venus as an evening star is Hesperus and it was then, traditionally, said to be sacred to lovers. Evening-star people tend to be easy-going and are open to negotiation, conciliation and making peace. If you are an evening-star Venus person, your best times in relationship and business affairs are said to be when Venus can be seen, jewel-like, in the western sky after the Sun has set.

Because the orbit of Venus is so close to the Sun, your Venus can only be in one of five signs. You have a morning-star Venus if your Venus is in one of the two signs that come before your Sun sign in the zodiac. You have an evening-star Venus if your Venus is in either of the two signs that follow your Sun sign. If you have Venus in the same sign as your Sun, you could be either, depending on whether your Venus is ahead or behind your Sun. (You can find out which at the author's website www.janeridderpatrick.com.)

If you don't yet know your Venus sign, you might like to read through all of the following descriptions and see if you can guess what it is. You can find out for sure on pp.116–18.

At the beginning of each section are the names of some well-known Aquarians with that particular Venus sign. You can find out more about them in Chapter Ten, Famous Aquarius Birthdays.

Sun in Aquarius with Venus in Aries

| Jennifer Aniston | Charles Darwin | Mia Farrow |
| Betty Friedan | Abraham Lincoln | Bob Marley |

Venus in Aries is direct and to the point. When you want someone, you want them urgently – and instantly – and you're unlikely to have much hesitation about letting them know your desires. The thrill of the chase turns you on, and the harder it is to win the prize, the more fired up you become. But if the tables are turned and you become the hunted, you're liable to do a runner. With little subtlety or bashfulness, but naivety in buckets, you'll plunge straight in on an overwhelming impulse, giving no thought for the practicalities of the situation, and sometimes get your fingers burnt. Bob Marley had eleven children by eight different mothers. An incurable romantic, no matter how often love has let you down, the hope that this time you have found the Real Thing will never desert you.

Feisty, colourful and independent partners, who may also be demanding or wilful, turn you on. You'll probably try to dominate them but any partner who would submit to your control would lose your respect instantly. Conflict, healthy or otherwise, is likely to feature in your relationships, with competition between you and your lovers, or rivals, for top of the heap. You are well able to stand up for yourself and have no hesitation about doing so if need be. If you're in a committed relationship, it's essential that you find some kind of suitable outlet for your restless and dynamic energies. New projects, especially ones you can pour your heart into and that will stretch you beyond your limits, are ideal for you. As you enjoy a good fight, and risk and danger put a spring in your step, you'll often go out of your way to attract them.

Sun in Aquarius with Venus in Sagittarius

| Havelock Ellis | Germaine Greer | Eartha Kitt |
| Claire Rayner | Kirsty Wark | Boris Yeltsin |

Sagittarius is the sign of teaching and preaching, advising and adventure, travel and foreign culture and, in one form or another, those are the areas where you'll find your bliss. You have opinions – frequently unconventional or controversial ones – and it's unlikely that you'll keep them to yourself. You make an inspiring teacher and, with your gift for injecting optimism and faith and bringing out the best in people, you often leave the lives of those you have touched the better for your having passed through. Tact, however, may not always be your strong point.

Foreigners or foreign places could pull you strongly. Eartha Kitt, despite coming from a poverty-stricken background, went on to become an international star, fluent in six languages – and used all of them to broadcast her feminist views. Your partner may be connected with travelling, sport, publishing or the legal profession, and so could you. Relationships where you learn from, or teach, others help you to develop wisdom and little stirs you up as much as discussing the meaning of life and your own part in it. Being a free spirit, you hate to be tied down and it would be hard for you to stay committed to a partner who does not either share your beliefs and passionate causes or, alternatively, allows you plenty of freedom to explore these interests alone. Havelock Ellis published, during the prudish Victorian era, *Studies in the Psychology of Sex*, the first detached treatment of the subject, free from guilt, a seven-volume work based partly on his own experiences. It was banned in Britain. His biography reports, coyly, that he had a number of female followers throughout his life.

Sun in Aquarius with Venus in Capricorn

Eva Braun	Zsa Zsa Gabor	Somerset Maugham
Paul Newman	Sophie, Countess of Wessex	Jerry Springer

Your self-esteem is linked to the successful achievement of your goals, and lasting happiness comes when you find a respected position in the community where you can make some substantial contribution, preferably one that will benefit posterity. Jerry Springer was once a serious politician and Mayor of Cincinnati. Partners who bring you difficulties, hardship or increased responsibilities may attract you like a magnet, as you love hard work and doing your duty. You, or your partner, can be phenomenally hard-working and enjoy breaking into the establishment, if you haven't been born into it. You may be drawn to partners who are much younger or older, or who are of a different status or station in life from you – usually higher.

With your appreciation of traditional values, you may prefer a partner who is either well-known or established in their field. When it comes to long-term relationships, you might not be the most romantic creature on the planet. You could take a long time making up your mind before tying the knot. That can be a great advantage, as you'll go into contracts with your eyes wide open, and so any partnership, either business or romantic, has a good chance of enduring. Paul Newman has been married to Joanne Woodward since 1958. Others with this combination have a business-like approach to relating, and an eye for the main chance, believing that if they do marry it might as well be at the top rather than the bottom of whatever ladder they're climbing. Nine-times-married actress Zsa Zsa Gabor also claims to be an excellent housekeeper. As she says, when she leaves a man, she keeps his house.

Sun in Aquarius with Venus in Aquarius

Robert Burns	Lord Byron	Joyce Grenfell
Barry Humphries	Yoko Ono	Oprah Winfrey

Powerful emotions coming towards you, especially of the dark and dangerous kind, and too much intimacy, make you dive for cover, though if you are well-shielded from their impact, you can enjoy studying and theorising about them. Your natural reserve can sometimes be mistaken for aloofness and disinterest, but you are far from cold. Friends mean a great deal to you and you could go to extraordinary lengths to help if they are ever in trouble. Being part of a group that's on your wavelength can bring you happiness and opportunities for lasting love. For a long-term commitment, a like-minded partner who shares your ideas, and ideals, is a must. You've an unselfish streak when it comes to money and could be attracted to contributing to unusual good causes.

Intellectual companionship and social experimentation suit you more than all-consuming passion. You don't give a fig what others think, and with your innate sense of perversity, may delight in shocking just for the sheer hell of it. Barry Humphries' alter ego, Dame Edna Everage, has an outrageous dress sense and a mouth to match. The love lives of Lord Byron and Robert Burns were active and varied, and they created scandal and controversy wherever they appeared. Both, too, supported revolutionary movements.

Being and staying at the cutting edge of your profession could bring you lasting happiness and satisfaction. You are likely to be skilled at networking and even if you never see people you care about for years on end, or they live at the opposite side of the world, you will still feel connected. Your friends stay your friends, for it is the meeting of minds that matters, not their physical presence in the same room.

Sun in Aquarius with Venus in Pisces

| Helen Gurley Brown | Colette | Charles Dickens |
| Thomas Edison | Vanessa Redgrave | John Travolta |

A powerful imagination is one of your greatest assets. More than any other Aquarian, you have a romantic streak that loves mushy love stories where the power of unselfish love triumphs over all adversity. Your dream of finding perfect bliss in the fusion of two hearts beating as one could cause you a heartache or two, until you reconcile your high ideals with human nature as it really is. You may be drawn to trying to rescue people who are damaged or emotionally unavailable. Alternatively, you could have long-lasting relationships with partners in films or advertising, art or music, spirituality or the caring professions, or be involved in those fields yourself.

Fleetingly, you can fall in love with, or see something utterly divine in, just about everyone you meet. You may need to check a tendency to confuse pity and sympathy with love, or be led astray by a hard-luck story or a good seductive line. Your heart is moved by suffering and vulnerability, and you may be drawn to causes that champion the underdog. Even if you are not conventionally beautiful, you have a glamour that can weave erotic spells, tapping into other people's fantasies and making the most unlikely people fall in love with you. The French writer Colette had an extraordinary love life, with both men and women. She had a five-year affair with her stepson, 30 years her junior, finally finding the love of her life at 53 with a man of 36. You are capable of devoted, sometimes self-sacrificial, love and there can be an idealistic and spiritual component in the quality of your affections. At its highest level, you'll find deep satisfaction in serving others unselfishly.

TEN

Famous Aquarius Birthdays

FIND OUT WHO SHARES YOUR MOON, MERCURY AND VENUS SIGNS, and any challenging Sun aspects, and see what they have done with the material they were born with. Notice how often it is not just the personalities of the people themselves but the roles of actors, characters of authors and works of artists that reflect their astrological make-up. In reading standard biographies, I've been constantly astounded – and, of course, delighted – at how often phrases used to describe individuals could have been lifted straight from their astrological profiles. Check it out yourself!

A few people below have been given a choice of two Moons. This is because the Moon changed sign on the day that they were born and no birth time was available. You may be able to guess which one is correct if you read the descriptions of the Moon signs in Chapter Seven.

20 January
1965 Sophie Rhys-Jones, Countess of Wessex and wife of Prince Edward
Sun aspects: none
Moon: Virgo   Mercury: Capricorn   Venus: Capricorn

21 January
1905 Christian Dior, fashion designer
Sun aspects: none
Moon: Cancer   Mercury: Capricorn   Venus: Pisces

22 January
1788 George Gordon, Lord Byron, romantic revolutionary poet with scandalous love life
Sun aspects: Uranus
Moon: Cancer   Mercury: Capricorn   Venus: Aquarius

23 January
1910 Django Reinhardt, vibrantly exciting gypsy jazz musician
Sun aspects: none
Moon: Cancer   Mercury: Aquarius   Venus: Pisces

24 January
1862 Edith Wharton, American author and social observer, *The House of Mirth*
Sun aspects: Pluto
Moon: Scorpio   Mercury: Aquarius   Venus: Pisces

25 January
1759 Robert Burns, Scotland's national poet and ladies' man, *Tam O'Shanter*
Sun aspects: none
Moon: Sagittarius   Mercury: Capricorn   Venus: Aquarius

26 January
1925 Paul Newman, actor, *Butch Cassidy and the Sundance Kid*
Sun aspects: Saturn
Moon: Pisces   Mercury: Capricorn   Venus: Capricorn

27 January
1756 Wolfgang Amadeus Mozart, Austrian composer of genius
Sun aspects: Saturn, Neptune
Moon: Sagittarius   Mercury: Aquarius   Venus: Aquarius

28 January
1873 Gabrielle Colette, sensual French writer, *Chéri* and *Gigi*
Sun aspects: Uranus, Pluto
Moon: Aquarius   Mercury: Capricorn   Venus: Pisces

29 January
1954 Oprah Winfrey, inspirational American talk-show hostess
Sun aspects: Saturn
Moon: Sagittarius   Mercury: Aquarius   Venus: Aquarius

30 January
1937 Vanessa Redgrave, actress and political activist, *Mrs Dalloway*
Sun aspects: Uranus
Moon: Virgo   Mercury: Capricorn   Venus: Pisces

31 January
1923 Norman Mailer, writer and political protester, *The American Dream*
Sun aspects: Neptune
Moon: Cancer   Mercury: Aquarius   Venus: Sagittarius

1 February
1931 Boris Yeltsin, the first democratically elected Russian president
Sun aspects: none
Moon: Cancer   Mercury: Capricorn   Venus: Sagittarius

2 February
1882 James Joyce, Irish writer, *Portrait of the Artist as a Young Man*, *Ulysses*
Sun aspects: Saturn, Neptune
Moon: Leo   Mercury: Pisces   Venus: Aquarius

3 February
1809 Felix Mendelssohn, romantic composer, 'The Wedding March'
Sun aspects: Uranus
Moon: Virgo   Mercury: Aquarius   Venus: Pisces

4 February
1921 Betty Friedan, feminist writer, *The Feminine Mystique*
Sun aspects: Neptune
Moon: Capricorn   Mercury: Aquarius   Venus: Aries

5 February
1788 Sir Robert Peel, creator of the London 'bobbies' named after him
Sun aspects: Pluto
Moon: Capricorn/Aquarius   Mercury: Aquarius
Venus: Pisces

6 February
1911 Ronald Reagan, US president who helped end the cold war with Russia
Sun aspects: none
Moon: Taurus   Mercury: Capricorn   Venus: Pisces

7 February
1812 Charles Dickens, English author, *Oliver Twist*, *A Christmas Carol*
Sun aspects: Uranus
Moon: Sagittarius   Mercury: Capricorn   Venus: Pisces

8 February
1828 Jules Verne, French author, *Around the World in Eighty Days*
Sun aspects: none
Moon: Scorpio   Mercury: Aquarius   Venus: Pisces

9 February
1945 Mia Farrow, actress with 14 children, 10 adopted, *Rosemary's Baby*
Sun aspects: none
Moon: Capricorn   Mercury: Aquarius   Venus: Aries

10 February
1920 Alex Comfort, sexologist and bestselling author, *The Joy of Sex*
Sun aspects: none
Moon: Scorpio   Mercury: Aquarius   Venus: Capricorn

11 February
1847 Thomas Edison, prolific inventor, notably of the electric lightbulb
Sun aspects: Saturn, Neptune
Moon: Sagittarius   Mercury: Aquarius   Venus: Pisces

12 February
1809 Abraham Lincoln, US president who abolished slavery
Sun aspects: Saturn
Moon: Capricorn   Mercury: Pisces   Venus: Aries

13 February
1944 Jerry Springer, TV talk-show host and former Mayor of Cincinnati
Sun aspects: none
Moon: Libra   Mercury: Aquarius   Venus: Capricorn

14 February
1951 Kevin Keegan, England international footballer
Sun aspects: Pluto
Moon: Taurus/Gemini   Mercury: Aquarius   Venus: Pisces

15 February
1954 Matt Groening, cartoonist and creator of *The Simpsons*
Sun aspects: Pluto
Moon: Cancer/Leo   Mercury: Pisces   Venus: Pisces

16 February
1959 John McEnroe, temperamental and voluble tennis champion
Sun aspects: Pluto
Moon: Gemini   Mercury: Aquarius   Venus: Pisces

17 February
1934 Barry Humphries, entertainer and creator of Dame Edna Everage
Sun aspects: Saturn
Moon: Aries   Mercury: Pisces   Venus: Aquarius

18 February
1933 Yoko Ono, artist and widow of John Lennon
Sun aspects: Neptune
Moon: Sagittarius   Mercury: Pisces   Venus: Aquarius

19 February
1911 Merle Oberon, exotically beautiful actress, *Wuthering Heights*
Sun aspects: none
Moon: Scorpio   Mercury: Aquarius   Venus: Pisces

Other Aquarian people mentioned in this book
Alfred Adler, psychologist who studied individuals considered as different from others ☆ Jennifer Aniston, actress, Rachel in *Friends* ☆ Queen Beatrix of the Netherlands ☆ Michael Bentine, comedian, co-creator of the Goons ☆ Elizabeth Blackwell, America's first woman doctor ☆ Linda Blair, actress, *The Exorcist* ☆ Eva Braun, Hitler's mistress ☆ Bertolt Brecht, playwright, *Mother Courage* ☆ Helen Gurley Brown, editor-in-chief at *Cosmopolitan* magazine ☆ Lewis Carroll, mathematician and author, *Alice in Wonderland* ☆ Alice Cooper, rock musician, 'No

More Mr Nice Guy' ☆ Charles Darwin, naturalist, *The Origin of Species* ☆ Geena Davis, actress, *Thelma and Louise* ☆ James Dean, actor, *Rebel Without a Cause* ☆ Plácido Domingo, opera singer, one of the Three Tenors ☆ Isabelle Eberhardt, Victorian adventuress ☆ Havelock Ellis, sexologist, *The Erotic Rights of Women* ☆ W.C. Fields, actor, *My Little Chickadee* ☆ Gennifer Flowers, cabaret singer and Bill Clinton's former lover ☆ Betty Friedan, feminist, *The Feminine Mystique* ☆ Clark Gable, actor, *Gone With the Wind* ☆ Zsa Zsa Gabor, much-married actress and author, *How to Catch a Man* ☆ Germaine Greer, feminist, *Sex and Destiny: The Politics of Human Fertility* ☆ Joyce Grenfell, comedy actress, *St Trinians* ☆ Margaux Hemingway, actress and Faberge model, *Lipstick*, who died of an overdose ☆ Michael Hutchence, lead singer of INXS, engaged to Paula Yates, found dead in mysterious circumstances ☆ David Jason, actor, *A Touch of Frost* ☆ Virginia Johnson, sex therapist, *Human Sexual Response* ☆ Jerome Kern, composer, 'Smoke Gets in Your Eyes' ☆ Eartha Kitt, sultry actress and singer, 'Just an Old-Fashioned Girl' ☆ Gypsy Rose Lee, striptease artist ☆ Prue Leith, cookery school director and writer ☆ Jack Lemmon, actor, *Some Like it Hot* ☆ Charles Lindbergh, aviation hero whose baby son was kidnapped and killed ☆ Bob Marley, reggae musician, *Songs of Freedom* ☆ Somerset Maugham, author, *Of Human Bondage* ☆ Jeanne Moreau, actress, *Jules et Jim* ☆ Toni Morrison, Nobel Prize-winning author of African-American classics, *Tar Baby* ☆ Jack Nicklaus, golfer ☆ Thomas Paine, American revolutionary philosopher, *The Rights of Man* ☆ Jackson Pollock, avant-garde artist who threw paint at canvases ☆ Jacqueline du Pré, outstanding cellist who died of MS ☆ Lisa Marie Presley, reclusive daughter of Elvis Presley, briefly married to Michael Jackson and Nicolas Cage ☆ Mary Quant, fashion designer who shaped the 1960s ☆ François Rabelais, bawdy sixteenth-century French satirist, *Gargantua* ☆ Claire Rayner, agony aunt and patients' rights activist ☆ Oliver Reed, hell-raising actor, *Women in Love* ☆ Ruth Rendell, crime writer, creator of the Wexford mysteries ☆ Franklin D. Roosevelt, former US president, whose innovative 'New Deal' helped America recover from the Great Depression ☆ Patricia Routledge, actress who plays Hyacinth Bucket in *Keeping Up Appearances* ☆ Jane Seymour, actress, *Dr Quinn, Medicine Woman* ☆ Muriel Spark, author, *The Prime of Miss Jean Brodie* ☆ Henry Morton Stanley, Welsh explorer and journalist, *How I Found Livingstone* ☆ Princess Stephanie, daughter of Princess Grace and Prince Rainer of Monaco ☆ Sharon Tate, actress wife of Roman Polanski, murdered by the Manson 'family' ☆ Maria von Trapp, stepmother whose life inspired *The Sound of Music* ☆ John Travolta, actor and singer, *Grease, Pulp Fiction* ☆ Alice Walker, author, *The Color Purple* ☆ Kirsty Wark, TV presenter, *Newsnight* ☆ James Watt, engineer and inventor of the steam engine ☆ Ken Wilber, philosopher exploring the unity of science and religion, *No Boundary* ☆ Robbie Williams, singer, *Escapology* ☆ Norman Wisdom, slapstick actor and national comedy hero of Albania ☆ Virginia Woolf, author, *To The Lighthouse*.

ELEVEN

Finding your Sun, Moon, Mercury and Venus Signs

All of the astrological data in this book was calculated by Astrolabe, who also supply a wide range of astrological software. I am most grateful for their help and generosity.

ASTROLABE, PO Box 1750, Brewster, MA 02631, USA
w w w.alabe.com

PLEASE NOTE THAT ALL OF THE TIMES GIVEN ARE IN GREENWICH MEAN TIME (GMT). If you were born during British Summer Time (BST) you will need to subtract one hour from your birth time to convert it to GMT. If you were born outside of the British Isles, find the time zone of your place of birth and the number of hours it is different from GMT. Add the difference in hours if you were born west of the UK, and subtract the difference if you were born east of the UK to convert your birth time to GMT.

Your Sun Sign

Check your year of birth, and if you were born between the dates and times given the Sun was in Aquarius when you were born – confirming that you're an Aquarian. If you were born before the time on the date that Aquarius begins in your year, you are a Capricorn. If you were born after the time on the date Aquarius ends in your year, you are a Piscean.

Your Moon Sign

The Moon changes sign every two and a half days. To find your Moon sign, first find your year of birth. You will notice that in each year box there are three columns.

The second column shows the day of the month that the Moon changed sign, while the first column gives the abbreviation for the sign that the Moon entered on that date.

In the middle column, the month has been omitted, so that the dates run from, for example, 20 to 31 (January) and then from 1 to 19 (February).

In the third column, after the star, the time that the Moon changed sign on that day is given.

Look down the middle column of your year box to find your date of birth. If your birth date is given, look to the third column to find the time that the Moon changed sign. If you were born after that time, your Moon sign is given in the first column next to your birth date. If you were born before that time, your Moon sign is the one above the one next to your birth date.

If your birth date is not given, find the closest date before it. The sign shown next to that date is your Moon sign.

If you were born on a day that the Moon changed signs and you do not know your time of birth, try out both of that day's Moon signs and feel which one fits you best.

The abbreviations for the signs are as follows:

Aries – Ari   Taurus – Tau   Gemini – Gem   Cancer – Can
Leo – Leo   Virgo – Vir   Libra – Lib   Scorpio – Sco
Sagittarius – Sag   Capricorn – Cap   Aquarius – Aqu   Pisces – Pis

Your Mercury Sign

Find your year of birth and then the column in which your birthday falls. Look up to the top of the column to find your Mercury sign. You will see that some dates appear twice. This is because Mercury changed sign that day. If your birthday falls on one of these dates, try out both Mercury signs and see which one fits you best. If you know your birth time, you can find out for sure which Mercury sign is yours on my website – www.janeridderpatrick.com.

Your Venus Sign

Find your year of birth and then the column in which your birthday falls. Look up to the top of the column to find your Venus sign. Some dates have two possible signs. That's because Venus changed signs that day. Try them both out and see which fits you best. If the year you are interested in doesn't appear in the tables, or you have Venus in the same sign as your Sun and want to know whether you have a morning or evening star Venus, you can find the information on my website – www.janeridderpatrick.com.

♒ Aquarius Sun Tables ☉

YEAR	AQUARIUS BEGINS	AQUARIUS ENDS
1930	20 Jan 18.33	19 Feb 08.59
1931	21 Jan 00.17	19 Feb 14.40
1932	21 Jan 06.06	19 Feb 20.28
1933	20 Jan 11.52	19 Feb 02.16
1934	20 Jan 17.36	19 Feb 08.01
1935	20 Jan 23.28	19 Feb 13.52
1936	21 Jan 05.12	19 Feb 19.33
1937	20 Jan 11.01	19 Feb 01.20
1938	20 Jan 16.58	19 Feb 07.19
1939	20 Jan 22.50	19 Feb 13.09
1940	21 Jan 04.44	19 Feb 19.03
1941	20 Jan 10.33	19 Feb 00.56
1942	20 Jan 16.23	19 Feb 06.46
1943	20 Jan 22.18	19 Feb 12.40
1944	21 Jan 04.07	19 feb 18.27
1945	20 Jan 09.53	19 Feb 00.14
1946	20 Jan 15.44	19 Feb 06.08
1947	20 Jan 21.31	19 Feb 11.51
1948	21 Jan 03.18	19 Feb 17.36
1949	20 Jan 09.08	19 Feb 23.27
1950	20 Jan 14.59	19 Feb 05.17
1951	20 Jan 20.52	19 Feb 11.09
1952	21 Jan 02.38	19 Feb 16.56
1953	20 Jan 08.21	19 Feb 22.41
1954	20 Jan 14.11	19 Feb 04.32
1955	20 Jan 20.01	19 Feb 10.18
1956	21 Jan 01.48	19 Feb 16.04
1957	20 Jan 07.38	19 Feb 21.58
1958	20 Jan 13.28	19 feb 03.48
1959	20 Jan 19.18	19 Feb 09.37
1960	21 Jan 01.10	19 Feb 15.26
1961	20 Jan 07.01	19 Feb 21.16
1962	20 Jan 18.53	19 Feb 03.14
1963	20 Jan 18.53	19 Feb 09.08

YEAR	AQUARIUS BEGINS	AQUARIUS ENDS
1964	21 Jan 00.41	19 Feb 14.57
1965	20 Jan 06.28	19 Feb 20.47
1966	20 Jan 12.19	19 Feb 02.37
1967	20 Jan 18.07	19 Feb 08.23
1968	20 Jan 23.54	19 Feb 14.09
1969	20 Jan 05.38	19 Feb 14.09
1970	20 Jan 11.23	19 Feb 01.41
1971	20 Jan 17.12	19 Feb 07.27
1972	20 Jan 22.59	19 Feb 13.11
1973	20 Jan 04.48	19 Feb 19.01
1974	20 Jan 10.45	19 Feb 00.58
1975	20 Jan 16.36	19 Feb 06.49
1976	20 Jan 22.25	19 Feb 12.39
1977	20 Jan 04.14	18 Feb 18.30
1978	20 Jan 10.03	19 Feb 00.21
1979	20 Jan 15.59	19 Feb 06.13
1980	20 jan 21.48	19 Feb 12.01
1981	20 Jan 03.36	18 Feb 17.51
1982	20 Jan 09.30	18 Feb 23.46
1983	20 Jan 15.16	19 Feb 05.30
1984	20 Jan 21.05	19 Feb 11.16
1985	20 Jan 02.57	19 Feb 17.07
1986	20 Jan 08.46	19 Feb 22.57
1987	20 Jan 14.40	19 Feb 04.50
1988	20 Jan 20.24	19 Feb 10.35
1989	20 Jan 02.07	18 Feb 16.20
1990	20 Jan 08.01	19 Feb 22.14
1991	20 Jan 13.47	19 Feb 03.48
1992	20 Jan 19.32	19 Feb 09.43
1993	20 Jan 01.22	18 Feb 15.35
1994	20 Jan 07.07	18 Feb 15.35
1995	20 Jan 13.00	19 Feb 03.10
1996	20 Jan 18.52	19 Feb 09.00
1997	20 Jan 00.42	18 Feb 14.51
1998	20 Jan 06.46	18 Feb 20.54
1999	20 Jan 12.37	19 Feb 02.46
2000	20 Jan 18.23	19 Feb 08.33

Aquarius – Finding Your Moon Sign ☽

1930
Sco	21	*14:26
Sag	23	*23:56
Cap	26	*11:53
Aqu	29	*00:34
Pis	31	*12:58
Ari	3	*00:22
Tau	5	*09:47
Gem	7	*16:07
Can	9	*18:54
Leo	11	*19:00
Vir	13	*18:14
Lib	15	*18:50
Sco	17	*22:46

1931
Pis	21	*10:55
Ari	23	*23:54
Tau	26	*12:08
Gem	28	*21:16
Can	31	*02:07
Leo	2	*03:23
Vir	4	*02:56
Lib	6	*02:55
Sco	8	*05:04
Sag	10	*10:22
Cap	12	*18:39
Aqu	15	*05:14
Pis	17	*17:23

1932
Can	21	*04:21
Leo	23	*09:38
Vir	25	*12:46
Lib	27	*15:07
Sco	29	*17:43
Sag	31	*21:07
Cap	3	*01:39
Aqu	5	*07:48
Pis	7	*16:15
Ari	10	*03:17
Tau	12	*16:04
Gem	15	*04:27
Can	17	*14:01
Leo	19	*19:48

1933
Sag	21	*10:54
Cap	23	*12:17
Aqu	25	*13:57
Pis	27	*17:31
Ari	30	*00:22
Tau	1	*10:40
Gem	3	*23:04
Can	6	*11:12
Leo	8	*21:15
Vir	11	*04:42
Lib	13	*09:58
Sco	15	*13:45
Sag	17	*16:42
Cap	19	*19:22

1934
Ari	20	*01:29
Tau	22	*08:26
Gem	24	*18:54
Can	27	*07:23
Leo	29	*20:11
Vir	1	*07:59
Lib	3	*17:59
Sco	6	*01:30
Sag	8	*06:14
Cap	10	*08:22
Aqu	12	*08:57
Pis	14	*09:27
Ari	16	*11:40
Tau	18	*17:03

♒ Aquarius – Finding Your Moon Sign ☽

1935		
Vir	22	*07:19
Lib	24	*19:58
Sco	27	*06:45
Sag	29	*14:09
Cap	31	*17:47
Aqu	2	*18:25
Pis	4	*17:46
Ari	6	*17:48
Tau	8	*20:23
Gem	11	*02:36
Can	13	*12:24
Leo	16	*00:35
Vir	18	*13:32

1936		
Cap	21	*22:17
Aqu	24	*02:01
Pis	26	*03:34
Ari	28	*04:35
Tau	30	*06:37
Gem	1	*10:39
Can	3	*16:58
Leo	6	*01:26
Vir	8	*11:48
Lib	10	*23:45
Sco	13	*12:23
Sag	15	*23:55
Cap	18	*08:20

1937		
Gem	21	*23:53
Can	24	*02:38
Leo	26	*06:07
Vir	28	*11:31
Lib	30	*19:49
Sco	2	*07:10
Sag	4	*19:58
Cap	7	*07:33
Aqu	9	*15:59
Pis	11	*21:09
Ari	14	*00:11
Tau	16	*02:34
Gem	18	*05:22

1938		
Lib	20	*18:27
Sco	23	*02:55
Sag	25	*14:51
Cap	28	*03:57
Aqu	30	*15:59
Pis	2	*01:57
Ari	4	*09:53
Tau	6	*15:57
Gem	8	*20:07
Can	10	*22:25
Leo	12	*23:33
Vir	15	*00:57
Lib	17	*04:28
Sco	19	*11:38

1939		
Aqu	20	*14:14
Pis	23	*02:50
Ari	25	*14:41
Tau	28	*00:27
Gem	30	*06:49
Can	1	*09:20
Leo	3	*09:05
Vir	5	*08:02
Lib	7	*08:30
Sco	9	*12:23
Sag	11	*20:24
Cap	14	*07:41
Aqu	16	*20:21
Pis	19	*08:51

≋ Aquarius – Finding Your Moon Sign ☽

1940

Gem	20	*10:30
Can	22	*15:33
Leo	24	*17:10
Vir	26	*17:11
Lib	28	*17:42
Sco	30	*20:18
Sag	2	*01:36
Cap	4	*09:27
Aqu	6	*19:21
Pis	9	*06:58
Ari	11	*19:49
Tau	14	*08:35
Gem	16	*19:09
Can	19	*01:44

1941

Sco	20	*10:03
Sag	22	*13:16
Cap	24	*17:01
Aqu	26	*22:06
Pis	29	*05:34
Ari	31	*16:02
Tau	3	*04:40
Gem	5	*17:09
Can	8	*02:56
Leo	10	*09:06
Vir	12	*12:20
Lib	14	*14:07
Sco	16	*15:52
Sag	18	*18:36

1942

Ari	21	*13:09
Tau	23	*23:19
Gem	26	*11:43
Can	29	*00:02
Leo	31	*10:36
Vir	2	*18:57
Lib	5	*01:17
Sco	7	*05:55
Sag	9	*09:06
Cap	11	*11:18
Aqu	13	*13:27
Pis	15	*16:50
Ari	17	*22:47

1943

Leo	21	*09:43
Vir	23	*22:02
Lib	26	*08:46
Sco	28	*16:50
Sag	30	*21:32
Cap	1	*23:14
Aqu	3	*23:10
Pis	5	*23:08
Ari	8	*01:01
Tau	10	*06:17
Gem	12	*15:25
Can	15	*03:24
Leo	17	*16:18

1944

Sag	21	*03:52
Cap	23	*07:26
Aqu	25	*08:09
Pis	27	*07:47
Ari	29	*08:15
Tau	31	*11:07
Gem	2	*17:17
Can	5	*02:40
Leo	7	*14:20
Vir	10	*03:07
Lib	12	*15:54
Sco	15	*03:23
Sag	17	*12:13
Cap	19	*17:32

≋ Aquarius – Finding Your Moon Sign ☽

1945		
Tau	20	*22:48
Gem	23	*02:35
Can	25	*08:05
Leo	27	*15:33
Vir	30	*01:09
Lib	1	*12:45
Sco	4	*01:21
Sag	6	*12:56
Cap	8	*21:28
Aqu	11	*02:10
Pis	13	*03:52
Ari	15	*04:12
Tau	17	*05:05
Gem	19	*08:01

1946		
Vir	20	*00:41
Lib	22	*08:32
Sco	24	*19:40
Sag	27	*08:26
Cap	29	*20:17
Aqu	1	*05:23
Pis	3	*11:31
Ari	5	*15:37
Tau	7	*18:46
Gem	9	*21:45
Can	12	*00:58
Leo	14	*04:50
Vir	16	*10:03
Lib	18	*17:36

1947		
Aqu	22	*05:36
Pis	24	*16:22
Ari	27	*01:09
Tau	29	*07:44
Gem	31	*11:50
Can	2	*13:37
Leo	4	*14:01
Vir	6	*14:42
Lib	8	*17:39
Sco	11	*00:29
Sag	13	*11:16
Cap	16	*00:11
Aqu	18	*12:37

1948		
Gem	21	*21:00
Can	23	*23:21
Leo	25	*22:59
Vir	27	*21:56
Lib	29	*22:30
Sco	1	*02:28
Sag	3	*10:26
Cap	5	*21:29
Aqu	8	*09:59
Pis	10	*22:36
Ari	13	*10:36
Tau	15	*21:07
Gem	18	*04:55

1949		
Sco	21	*12:00
Sag	23	*17:09
Cap	26	*00:22
Aqu	28	*09:26
Pis	30	*20:26
Ari	2	*09:04
Tau	4	*21:56
Gem	7	*08:39
Can	9	*15:21
Leo	11	*18:00
Vir	13	*18:05
Lib	15	*17:43
Sco	17	*18:53
Sag	19	*22:50

≋ Aquarius – Finding Your Moon Sign ☽

1950		
Pis	20	*18:41
Ari	23	*04:37
Tau	25	*17:07
Gem	28	*05:42
Can	30	*15:49
Leo	1	*22:32
Vir	4	*02:36
Lib	6	*05:18
Sco	8	*07:50
Sag	10	*10:51
Cap	12	*14:44
Aqu	14	*19:57
Pis	17	*03:11
Ari	19	*13:01

1951		
Can	20	*13:05
Leo	23	*00:10
Vir	25	*09:25
Lib	27	*16:45
Sco	29	*22:02
Sag	1	*01:15
Cap	3	*02:52
Aqu	5	*04:03
Pis	7	*06:28
Ari	9	*11:43
Tau	11	*20:33
Gem	14	*08:18
Can	16	*20:50
Leo	19	*08:00

1952		
Sco	20	*07:43
Sag	22	*12:20
Cap	24	*13:38
Aqu	26	*13:06
Pis	28	*12:46
Ari	30	*14:33
Tau	1	*19:51
Gem	4	*04:55
Can	6	*16:44
Leo	9	*05:35
Vir	11	*18:01
Lib	14	*04:59
Sco	16	*13:43
Sag	18	*19:41

1953		
Tau	22	*02:21
Gem	24	*08:21
Can	26	*17:06
Leo	29	*04:06
Vir	31	*16:35
Lib	3	*05:31
Sco	5	*17:20
Sag	8	*02:18
Cap	10	*07:31
Aqu	12	*09:15
Pis	14	*08:57
Ari	16	*08:31
Tau	18	*09:51

1954		
Vir	21	*14:14
Lib	24	*01:30
Sco	26	*14:03
Sag	29	*01:41
Cap	31	*10:25
Aqu	2	*15:37
Pis	4	*18:03
Ari	6	*19:14
Tau	8	*20:47
Gem	10	*23:54
Can	13	*05:10
Leo	15	*12:35
Vir	17	*22:00

♒ Aquarius – Finding Your Moon Sign ☽

1955		
Cap	21	*09:08
Aqu	23	*18:58
Pis	26	*02:10
Ari	28	*07:19
Tau	30	*11:05
Gem	1	*14:02
Can	3	*16:36
Leo	5	*19:28
Vir	7	*23:43
Lib	10	*06:33
Sco	12	*16:38
Sag	15	*05:07
Cap	17	*17:34

1956		
Tau	20	*23:09
Gem	23	*03:04
Can	25	*04:19
Leo	27	*04:06
Vir	29	*04:17
Lib	31	*06:56
Sco	2	*13:34
Sag	5	*00:13
Cap	7	*13:08
Aqu	10	*01:51
Pis	12	*12:51
Ari	14	*21:47
Tau	17	*04:48
Gem	19	*09:49

1957		
Lib	20	*12:56
Sco	22	*17:02
Sag	25	*00:52
Cap	27	*11:32
Aqu	29	*23:41
Pis	1	*12:20
Ari	4	*00:41
Tau	6	*11:36
Gem	8	*19:33
Can	10	*23:37
Leo	13	*00:17
Vir	14	*23:17
Lib	16	*22:50
Sco	19	*01:07

1958		
Pis	22	*09:42
Ari	24	*22:03
Tau	27	*10:55
Gem	29	*21:45
Can	1	*04:39
Leo	3	*07:37
Vir	5	*08:10
Lib	7	*08:23
Sco	9	*10:03
Sag	11	*14:12
Cap	13	*20:55
Aqu	16	*05:51
Pis	18	*16:39

1959		
Can	22	*04:46
Leo	24	*12:12
Vir	26	*17:13
Lib	28	*20:53
Sco	31	*00:05
Sag	2	*03:10
Cap	4	*06:28
Aqu	6	*10:40
Pis	8	*16:50
Ari	11	*01:55
Tau	13	*13:47
Gem	16	*02:38
Can	18	*13:49

Aquarius – Finding Your Moon Sign ☽

1960		
Sco	21	*13:58
Sag	23	*17:02
Cap	25	*17:59
Aqu	27	*18:18
Pis	29	*19:57
Ari	1	*00:40
Tau	3	*09:16
Gem	5	*20:58
Can	8	*09:36
Leo	10	*21:07
Vir	13	*06:34
Lib	15	*13:54
Sco	17	*19:23
Sag	19	*23:11

1961		
Ari	21	*04:27
Tau	23	*09:52
Gem	25	*18:50
Can	28	*06:21
Leo	30	*19:04
Vir	2	*07:48
Lib	4	*19:26
Sco	7	*04:50
Sag	9	*10:59
Cap	11	*13:49
Aqu	13	*14:14
Pis	15	*13:53
Ari	17	*14:41
Tau	19	*18:21

1962		
Leo	20	*17:49
Vir	23	*05:53
Lib	25	*18:51
Sco	28	*06:53
Sag	30	*15:58
Cap	1	*21:08
Aqu	3	*22:55
Pis	5	*22:52
Ari	7	*22:51
Tau	10	*00:35
Gem	12	*05:18
Can	14	*13:20
Leo	17	*00:04
Vir	19	*12:26

1963		
Sag	20	*14:19
Cap	22	*23:22
Aqu	25	*05:13
Pis	27	*08:34
Ari	29	*10:43
Tau	31	*12:55
Gem	2	*16:03
Can	4	*20:40
Leo	7	*03:06
Vir	9	*11:36
Lib	11	*22:18
Sco	14	*10:38
Sag	16	*22:56
Cap	19	*08:59

1964		
Tau	22	*03:22
Gem	24	*06:04
Can	26	*07:51
Leo	28	*09:45
Vir	30	*13:09
Lib	1	*19:25
Sco	4	*05:12
Sag	6	*17:35
Cap	9	*06:10
Aqu	11	*16:38
Pis	14	*00:07
Ari	16	*05:09
Tau	18	*08:44

♒ Aquarius – Finding Your Moon Sign ☽

1965		
Lib	21	*20:28
Sco	24	*03:01
Sag	26	*13:32
Cap	29	*02:21
Aqu	31	*15:17
Pis	3	*02:55
Ari	5	*12:42
Tau	7	*20:23
Gem	10	*01:35
Can	12	*04:13
Leo	14	*04:54
Vir	16	*05:05
Lib	18	*06:45

1966		
Aqu	21	*13:26
Pis	24	*01:58
Ari	26	*14:32
Tau	29	*01:41
Gem	31	*09:42
Can	2	*13:39
Leo	4	*14:13
Vir	6	*13:11
Lib	8	*12:51
Sco	10	*15:15
Sag	12	*21:33
Cap	15	*07:25
Aqu	17	*19:25

1967		
Gem	21	*10:36
Can	23	*17:50
Leo	25	*21:19
Vir	27	*22:35
Lib	29	*23:33
Sco	1	*01:44
Sag	3	*05:55
Cap	5	*12:10
Aqu	7	*20:17
Pis	10	*06:18
Ari	12	*18:16
Tau	15	*07:18
Gem	17	*19:15

1968		
Lib	20	*12:46
Sco	22	*16:27
Sag	24	*19:23
Cap	26	*21:57
Aqu	29	*01:06
Pis	31	*06:15
Ari	2	*14:40
Tau	5	*02:15
Gem	7	*15:08
Can	10	*02:33
Leo	12	*10:48
Vir	14	*16:02
Lib	16	*19:21
Sco	18	*21:59

1969		
Pis	20	*09:21
Ari	22	*13:44
Tau	24	*22:13
Gem	27	*09:53
Can	29	*22:35
Leo	1	*10:28
Vir	3	*20:40
Lib	6	*04:59
Sco	8	*11:17
Sag	10	*15:22
Cap	12	*17:28
Aqu	14	*18:30
Pis	16	*20:03
Ari	18	*23:49

≋ Aquarius – Finding Your Moon Sign ☽

1970

Leo	22	*08:40
Vir	24	*21:32
Lib	27	*09:41
Sco	29	*19:33
Sag	1	*01:48
Cap	3	*04:20
Aqu	5	*04:19
Pis	7	*03:37
Ari	9	*04:17
Tau	11	*07:59
Gem	13	*15:29
Can	16	*02:17
Leo	18	*14:53

1971

Sag	22	*05:15
Cap	24	*10:31
Aqu	26	*12:35
Pis	28	*13:01
Ari	30	*13:36
Tau	1	*15:49
Gem	3	*20:35
Can	6	*04:07
Leo	8	*14:06
Vir	11	*01:57
Lib	13	*14:49
Sco	16	*03:21
Sag	18	*13:44

1972

Ari	21	*02:34
Tau	23	*05:17
Gem	25	*08:13
Can	27	*12:02
Leo	29	*17:21
Vir	1	*00:56
Lib	3	*11:07
Sco	5	*23:17
Sag	8	*11:37
Cap	10	*21:48
Aqu	13	*04:35
Pis	15	*08:10
Ari	17	*09:50
Tau	19	*11:11

1973

Vir	21	*02:24
Lib	23	*08:16
Sco	25	*17:51
Sag	28	*06:10
Cap	30	*18:53
Aqu	2	*05:55
Pis	4	*14:21
Ari	6	*20:28
Tau	9	*00:53
Gem	11	*04:09
Can	13	*06:44
Leo	15	*09:12
Vir	17	*12:31
Lib	19	*17:58

1974

Cap	20	*15:47
Aqu	23	*04:49
Pis	25	*17:00
Ari	28	*03:31
Tau	30	*11:40
Gem	1	*16:52
Can	3	*19:05
Leo	5	*19:11
Vir	7	*18:51
Lib	9	*20:10
Sco	12	*00:59
Sag	14	*10:01
Cap	16	*22:15
Aqu	19	*11:20

♒ Aquarius – Finding Your Moon Sign ☽

1975		
Tau	20	*15:20
Gem	22	*23:21
Can	25	*03:19
Leo	27	*03:59
Vir	29	*03:13
Lib	31	*03:14
Sco	2	*05:53
Sag	4	*12:11
Cap	6	*21:42
Aqu	9	*09:16
Pis	11	*21:45
Ari	14	*10:21
Tau	16	*22:08
Gem	19	*07:34

1976		
Lib	21	*15:10
Sco	23	*17:47
Sag	25	*21:51
Cap	28	*03:24
Aqu	30	*10:34
Pis	1	*19:46
Ari	4	*07:17
Tau	6	*20:12
Gem	9	*08:15
Can	11	*16:58
Leo	13	*21:31
Vir	15	*22:58
Lib	17	*23:14

1977		
Pis	21	*19:30
Ari	24	*03:20
Tau	26	*14:41
Gem	29	*03:36
Can	31	*15:19
Leo	3	*00:10
Vir	5	*06:16
Lib	7	*10:35
Sco	9	*14:03
Sag	11	*17:10
Cap	13	*20:13
Aqu	15	*23:45
Pis	18	*04:44

1978		
Can	21	*11:50
Leo	24	*00:01
Vir	26	*10:55
Lib	28	*20:07
Sco	31	*03:02
Sag	2	*07:12
Cap	4	*08:49
Aqu	6	*09:04
Pis	8	*09:48
Ari	10	*12:57
Tau	12	*19:50
Gem	15	*06:24
Can	17	*18:55

1979		
Sco	21	*09:49
Sag	23	*16:06
Cap	25	*18:27
Aqu	27	*18:11
Pis	29	*17:25
Ari	31	*18:11
Tau	2	*22:04
Gem	5	*05:33
Can	7	*16:05
Leo	10	*04:25
Vir	12	*17:17
Lib	15	*05:36
Sco	17	*16:11
Sag	19	*23:49

≋ Aquarius – Finding Your Moon Sign ☽

1980			1981			1982			1983			1984		
Pis	20	*03:32	Leo	20	*07:21	Cap	22	*07:50	Tau	22	*02:34	Vir	20	*17:35
Ari	22	*04:51	Vir	22	*14:03	Aqu	24	*19:24	Gem	24	*07:39	Lib	22	*18:06
Tau	24	*07:31	Lib	24	*23:45	Pis	27	*04:48	Can	26	*09:27	Sco	24	*21:04
Gem	26	*12:11	Sco	27	*11:48	Ari	29	*11:57	Leo	28	*09:09	Sag	27	*03:13
Can	28	*19:02	Sag	30	*00:10	Tau	31	*17:03	Vir	30	*08:35	Cap	29	*12:12
Leo	31	*04:08	Cap	1	*10:35	Gem	2	*20:19	Lib	1	*09:48	Aqu	31	*23:11
Vir	2	*15:21	Aqu	3	*17:54	Can	4	*22:17	Sco	3	*14:33	Pis	3	*11:21
Lib	5	*04:04	Pis	5	*22:20	Leo	6	*23:50	Sag	5	*23:29	Ari	6	*00:03
Sco	7	*16:45	Ari	8	*01:01	Vir	9	*02:15	Cap	8	*11:33	Tau	8	*12:04
Sag	10	*03:18	Tau	10	*03:10	Lib	11	*07:02	Aqu	11	*00:40	Gem	10	*21:38
Cap	12	*10:10	Gem	12	*05:50	Sco	13	*15:16	Pis	13	*13:01	Can	13	*03:19
Aqu	14	*13:18	Can	14	*09:43	Sag	16	*02:45	Ari	15	*23:45	Leo	15	*05:08
Pis	16	*13:53	Leo	16	*15:10	Cap	18	*15:35	Tau	18	*08:29	Vir	17	*04:31
Ari	18	*13:42	Vir	18	*22:34							Lib	19	*03:39

☵ Aquarius – Finding Your Moon Sign ☽

1985

Aqu	21	*00:38
Pis	23	*09:02
Ari	25	*20:05
Tau	28	*08:53
Gem	30	*20:59
Can	2	*05:58
Leo	4	*11:00
Vir	6	*13:08
Lib	8	*14:10
Sco	10	*15:49
Sag	12	*19:08
Cap	15	*00:27
Aqu	17	*07:36
Pis	19	*16:38

1986

Gem	20	*16:11
Can	23	*04:14
Leo	25	*13:46
Vir	27	*20:50
Lib	30	*02:09
Sco	1	*06:19
Sag	3	*09:31
Cap	5	*12:01
Aqu	7	*14:35
Pis	9	*18:32
Ari	12	*01:21
Tau	14	*11:38
Gem	17	*00:16
Can	19	*12:38

1987

Lib	20	*11:08
Sco	22	*18:30
Sag	24	*22:34
Cap	26	*23:41
Aqu	28	*23:17
Pis	30	*23:25
Ari	2	*02:10
Tau	4	*08:53
Gem	6	*19:23
Can	9	*07:55
Leo	11	*20:20
Vir	14	*07:25
Lib	16	*16:44
Sco	19	*00:03

1988

Pis	21	*07:26
Ari	23	*08:31
Tau	25	*12:37
Gem	27	*20:02
Can	30	*06:11
Leo	1	*18:05
Vir	4	*06:54
Lib	6	*19:35
Sco	9	*06:41
Sag	11	*14:34
Cap	13	*18:36
Aqu	15	*19:24
Pis	17	*18:43
Ari	19	*18:35

1989

Leo	21	*18:02
Vir	24	*04:32
Lib	26	*17:01
Sco	29	*05:48
Sag	31	*16:29
Cap	2	*23:28
Aqu	5	*02:50
Pis	7	*03:51
Ari	9	*04:17
Tau	11	*05:44
Gem	13	*09:23
Can	15	*15:40
Leo	18	*00:33

≈≈≈ Aquarius – Finding Your Moon Sign ☽

1990		
Sag	21	*12:43
Cap	23	*23:26
Aqu	26	*07:24
Pis	28	*12:49
Ari	30	*16:33
Tau	1	*19:27
Gem	3	*22:12
Can	6	*01:27
Leo	8	*05:51
Vir	10	*12:13
Lib	12	*21:09
Sco	15	*08:34
Sag	17	*21:06

1991		
Ari	21	*03:26
Tau	23	*08:59
Gem	25	*12:05
Can	27	*13:22
Leo	29	*14:03
Vir	31	*15:44
Lib	2	*20:02
Sco	5	*04:01
Sag	7	*15:23
Cap	10	*04:15
Aqu	12	*16:16
Pis	15	*01:57
Ari	17	*09:10
Tau	19	*14:23

1992		
Vir	21	*22:22
Lib	23	*23:43
Sco	26	*04:32
Sag	28	*13:20
Cap	31	*01:07
Aqu	2	*14:08
Pis	5	*02:50
Ari	7	*14:14
Tau	9	*23:34
Gem	12	*06:07
Can	14	*09:29
Leo	16	*10:14
Vir	18	*09:46

1993		
Cap	20	*02:46
Aqu	22	*13:00
Pis	25	*00:47
Ari	27	*13:27
Tau	30	*01:36
Gem	1	*11:13
Can	3	*16:55
Leo	5	*18:50
Vir	7	*18:28
Lib	9	*17:58
Sco	11	*19:23
Sag	14	*00:08
Cap	16	*08:20
Aqu	18	*19:05

1994		
Gem	22	*09:33
Can	24	*18:54
Leo	27	*00:36
Vir	29	*03:38
Lib	31	*05:33
Sco	2	*07:49
Sag	4	*11:14
Cap	6	*16:01
Aqu	8	*22:17
Pis	11	*06:22
Ari	13	*16:49
Tau	16	*05:19
Gem	18	*18:05

♒ Aquarius – Finding Your Moon Sign ☽

1995			1996			1997			1998			1999			2000		
Vir	19	*11:38	Aqu	20	*13:14	Can	20	*20:28	Sco	20	*18:34	Pis	20	*03:39	Leo	21	*03:58
Lib	21	*17:53	Pis	22	*13:02	Leo	23	*07:49	Sag	23	*05:24	Ari	22	*08:24	Vir	23	*05:07
Sco	23	*22:31	Ari	24	*15:37	Vir	25	*20:26	Cap	25	*12:37	Tau	24	*11:51	Lib	25	*09:10
Sag	26	*01:35	Tau	26	*22:17	Lib	28	*09:20	Aqu	27	*16:26	Gem	26	*14:29	Sco	27	*17:01
Cap	28	*03:26	Gem	29	*08:42	Sco	30	*20:47	Pis	29	*18:08	Can	28	*16:56	Sag	30	*04:17
Aqu	30	*05:03	Can	31	*21:10	Sag	2	*04:50	Ari	31	*19:20	Leo	30	*20:16	Cap	1	*17:09
Pis	1	*08:05	Leo	3	*09:45	Cap	4	*08:43	Tau	2	*21:25	Vir	2	*01:38	Aqu	4	*05:30
Ari	3	*14:13	Vir	5	*21:21	Aqu	6	*09:20	Gem	5	*01:10	Lib	4	*09:56	Pis	6	*16:01
Tau	6	*00:09	Lib	8	*07:29	Pis	8	*08:33	Can	7	*06:57	Sco	6	*21:06	Ari	9	*00:16
Gem	8	*12:43	Sco	10	*15:34	Ari	10	*08:29	Leo	9	*14:57	Sag	9	*09:37	Tau	11	*06:20
Can	11	*01:16	Sag	12	*20:57	Tau	12	*10:57	Vir	12	*01:10	Cap	11	*21:09	Gem	13	*10:22
Leo	13	*11:30	Cap	14	*23:28	Gem	14	*16:53	Lib	14	*13:17	Aqu	14	*05:56	Can	15	*12:44
Vir	15	*18:51	Aqu	16	*23:59	Can	17	*02:13	Sco	17	*02:12	Pis	16	*11:38	Leo	17	*14:11
Lib	17	*23:59	Pis	19	*00:09	Leo	19	*13:52	Sag	19	*13:55	Ari	18	*15:05	Vir	19	*15:53

113

♒ Aquarius Mercury Signs ☿

YEAR	CAPRICORN	AQUARIUS	PISCES
1930	23 Jan–19 Feb	20 Jan–23 Jan	
1931	20 Jan–11 Feb	11 Feb–19 Feb	
1932	20 Jan–5 Feb	5 Feb–19 Feb	
1933	20 Jan–27 Jan	27 Jan–14 Feb	14 Feb–19 Feb
1934	20 Jan–6 Feb	6 Feb–19 Feb	
1935		20 Jan–1 Feb	1 Feb–15 Feb
		15 Feb–19 Feb	
1936		20 Jan–19 Feb	
1937	20 Jan–14 Feb	14 Feb–19 Feb	
1938	20 Jan–8 Feb	8 Feb–19 Feb	
1939	20 Jan–1 Feb	1 Feb–19 Feb	19 Feb
1940	20 Jan–25 Jan	25 Jan–11 Feb	11 Feb–19 Feb
1941		20 Jan–3 Feb	3 Feb–19 Feb
1942		20 Jan–19 Feb	
1943	27 Jan–15 Feb	20 Jan–27 Jan	
		15 Feb–19 Feb	
1944	20 Jan–12 Feb	12 Feb–19 Feb	
1945	20 Jan–5 Feb	5 Feb–19 Feb	
1946	20 Jan–29 Jan	29 Jan–15 Feb	15 Feb–19 Feb
1947	20 Jan–21 Jan	21 Jan–8 Feb	8 Feb–19 Feb
1948		20 Jan–2 Feb	2 Feb–19 Feb
1949		20 Jan–19 Feb	
1950	20 Jan–14 Feb	14 Feb–19 Feb	
1951	20 Jan–9 Feb	9 Feb–19 Feb	
1952	20 Jan–3 Feb	3 Feb–19 Feb	
1953	20 Jan–25 Jan	25 Jan–11 Feb	11 Feb–19 Feb
1954		20 Jan–4 Feb	4 Feb–19 Feb
1955		20 Jan–19 Feb	
1956	2 Feb–15 Feb	20 Jan–2 Feb	
		15 Feb–19 Feb	
1957	20 Jan–12 Feb	12 Feb–19 Feb	
1958	20 Jan–6 Feb	6 Feb–19 Feb	
1959	20 Jan–30 Jan	30 Jan–17 Feb	17 Feb–19 Feb
1960	20 Jan–23 Jan	23 Jan–9 Feb	9 Feb–19 Feb
1961		20 Jan–1 Feb	1 Feb–19 Feb
1962		20 Jan–19 Feb	
1963	20 Jan–15 Feb	20 Jan	
		15 Feb–19 Feb	
1964	20 Jan–10 Feb	10 Feb–19 Feb	
1965	20 Jan–3 Feb	3 Feb–19 Feb	

YEAR	CAPRICORN	AQUARIUS	PISCES
1966	20 Jan–27 Jan	27 Jan–13 Feb	13 Feb–19 Feb
1967		20 Jan–6 Feb	6 Feb–19 Feb
1968		20 Jan–1 Feb	1 Feb–11 Feb
		11 Feb–19 Feb	
1969		20 Jan–19 Feb	
1970	20 Jan–13 Feb	13 Feb–19 Feb	
1971	20 Jan–7 Feb	7 Feb–19 Feb	
1972	20 Jan–31 Jan	31 Jan–18 Feb	18 Feb–19 Feb
1973	20 Jan–23 Jan	23 Jan–9 Feb	9 Feb–19 Feb
1974		20 Jan–2 Feb	2 Feb–19 Feb
1975		20 Jan –19 Feb	
1976	25 Jan–15 Feb	20 Jan–25 Jan	15 Feb–19 Feb
1977	20 Jan–10 Feb	10 Feb–19 Feb	
1978	20 Jan–4 Feb	4 Feb–19 Feb	
1979	20 Jan–28 Jan	28 Jan–14 Feb	14 Feb–19 Feb
1980	20 Jan–21 Jan	21 Jan–7 Feb	7 Feb–19 Feb
1981		20 Jan–31 Jan	31 Jan–16 Feb
		16 Feb–19 Feb	
1982		20 Jan–19 Feb	
1983	20 Jan–14 Feb	14 Feb–19 Feb	
1984	20 Jan–9 Feb	9 Feb–19 Feb	
1985	20 Jan–1 Feb	1 Feb–18 Feb	18 Feb–19 Feb
1986	20 Jan–25 Jan	25 Jan–11 Feb	11 Feb–19 Feb
1987		20 Jan–4 Feb	4 Feb–19 Feb
1988		20 Jan–19 Feb	
1989	29 Jan–14 Feb	20 Jan–29 Jan	
		14 Feb–19 Feb	
1990	20 Jan–12 Feb	12 Feb–19 Feb	
1991	20 Jan–5 Feb	5 Feb–19 Feb	
1992	20 Jan–29 Jan	29 Jan–16 Feb	16 Feb–19 Feb
1993	20 Jan–21 Jan	21 Jan–7 Feb	7 Feb–19 Feb
1994		20 Jan–1 Feb	1 Feb–19 Feb
1995		20 Jan–19 Feb	
1996		20 Jan–15 Feb	15 Feb–19 Feb
1997	20 Jan–9 Feb	9 Feb–19 Feb	
1998	20 Jan–2 Feb	2 Feb–19 Feb	
1999	20 Jan–26 Jan	26 Jan–12 Feb	12 Feb–19 Feb
2000		20 Jan–5 Feb	5 Feb–19 Feb

≋ Aquarius Venus Signs ♀

YEAR	SAGITTARIUS	CAPRICORN	AQUARIUS	PISCES	ARIES
1930		20 Jan–24 Jan	24 Jan–16 Feb	16 Feb–19 Feb	
1931	20 Jan–6 Feb	6 Feb–19 Feb			
1932		20 Jan–7 Feb	7 Feb–19 Feb	20 Jan–12 Feb	12 Feb–19 Feb
1933			20 Jan–19 Feb		
1934			20 Jan–1 Feb	1 Feb–19 Feb	
1935	20 Jan–28 Jan	28 Jan–19 Feb			
1936				20 Jan–2 Feb	2 Feb–19 Feb
1937		20 Jan–23 Jan	23 Jan–16 Feb	16 Feb–19 Feb	
1938		6 Feb–19 Feb			
1939	20 Jan–6 Feb			20 Jan–12 Feb	12 Feb–19 Feb
1940		20 Jan–6 Feb	6 Feb–19 Feb		
1941			20 Jan–19 Feb		
1942			20 Jan–1 Feb	1 Feb–19 Feb	
1943	20 Jan–28 Jan	28 Jan–19 Feb			
1944			20 Jan–2 Feb	2 Feb–19 Feb	
1945		20 Jan–22 Jan	22 Jan–15 Feb	15 Feb–19 Feb	
1946	20 Jan–6 Feb	6 Feb–19 Feb			
1947				20 Jan–11 Feb	11 Feb–19 Feb
1948		20 Jan–6 Feb	6 Feb–19 Feb		
1949			20 Jan–19 Feb		
1950			20 Jan–31 Jan	31 Jan–19 Feb	
1951					

YEAR	SAGITTARIUS	CAPRICORN	AQUARIUS	PISCES	ARIES
1952	20 Jan–27 Jan	27 Jan–19 Feb		20 Jan–2 Feb	2 Feb–19 Feb
1953				15 Feb–19 Feb	
1954	20 Jan–6 Feb	20 Jan–22 Jan	22 Jan–15 Feb		
1955		6 Feb–19 Feb			11 Feb–19 Feb
1956		20 Jan–5 Feb		20 Jan–11 Feb	
1957			5 Feb–19 Feb		
1958			20 Jan–19 Feb		
1959			20 Jan–31 Jan		
1960	20 Jan–27 Jan	27 Jan–19 Feb		31 Jan–19 Feb	
1961					2 Feb–19 Feb
1962	20 Jan–5 Feb	20 Jan–21 Jan	21 Jan–14 Feb	20 Jan–2 Feb	
1963		5 Feb–19 Feb		14 Feb–19 Feb	10 Feb–19 Feb
1964				20 Jan–10 Feb	
1965		20 Jan–5 Feb	5 Feb–19 Feb		
1966		6 Feb–19 Feb	20 Jan–6 Feb		
1967	20 Jan–5 Feb	5 Feb–19 Feb	20 Jan–30 Jan	30 Jan–19 Feb	
1968					2 Feb–19 Feb
1969	20 Jan–5 Feb	20 Jan–21 Jan	21 Jan–14 Feb	20 Jan–2 Feb	
1970		5 Feb–19 Feb		14 Feb–19 Feb	
1971	20 Jan–5 Feb	5 Feb–19 Feb			10 Feb–19 Feb
1972					
1973		20 Jan–4 Feb	4 Feb–19 Feb	20 Jan–10 Feb	10 Feb–19 Feb
1974		29 Jan–19 Feb	20 Jan–29 Jan		
1975			20 Jan–30 Jan	30 Jan–19 Feb	
1976	20 Jan–26 Jan	26 Jan–19 Feb	19 Feb		

YEAR	SAGITTARIUS	CAPRICORN	AQUARIUS	PISCES	ARIES
1977		20 Jan–13 Feb	13 Feb–19 Feb	20 Jan–2 Feb	2 Feb–19 Feb
1978	20 Jan–5 Feb	5 Feb–19 Feb			
1979				20 Jan–9 Feb	9 Feb–19 Feb
1980		20 Jan–4 Feb	4 Feb–19 Feb		
1981		23 Jan–19 Feb	20 Jan–23 Jan		
1982			20 Jan–29 Jan		
1983		25 Jan–19 Feb	19 Feb	29 Jan–19 Feb	
1984	20 Jan–25 Jan				
1985		20 Jan	20 Jan–2 Feb	20 Jan–2 Feb	2 Feb–19 Feb
1986		5 Feb–19 Feb		2 Feb–19 Feb	
1987	20 Jan–5 Feb				
1988		20 Jan–3 Feb	3 Feb–19 Feb	20 Jan–9 Feb	9 Feb–19 Feb
1989		20 Jan–19 Feb			
1990			20 Jan–29 Jan		
1991		25 Jan–18 Feb	18 Feb–19 Feb	29 Jan–19 Feb	
1992	20 Jan–25 Jan		20 Jan–12 Feb	20 Jan–2 Feb	2 Feb–19 Feb
1993				12 Feb–19 Feb	
1994		4 Feb–19 Feb			
1995	20 Jan–4 Feb			20 Jan–9 Feb	9 Feb–19 Feb
1996		20 Jan–3 Feb	3 Feb–19 Feb		
1997		20 Jan–19 Feb			
1998					
1999		24 Jan–18 Feb	20 Jan–28 Jan	28 Jan–19 Feb	
2000	20 Jan–24 Jan		18 Feb–19 Feb		

The Aquarius Workbook

There are no right or wrong answers in this chapter. Its aim is to help you assess how you are doing with your life – in YOUR estimation – and to make the material of this book more personal and, I hope, more helpful for you.

1. The Aquarius in You
Which of the following Aquarius characteristics do you recognise in yourself?

altruistic	democratic	innovative
ethical	friendly	humanitarian
idealistic	nonconformist	progressive
rational	truthful	unselfish

2. In which situations do you find yourself acting like this?

_____

_____

3. When you are feeling vulnerable you may show some of the less constructive Aquarius traits. Do you recognise yourself in any of the following?

alienated	brusque	uncoordinated
rebellious	emotionally clumsy	impersonal
contrary	impractical	bloody-minded

What kind of situations trigger off this behaviour and what do you think might help you, in these situations, to respond more positively?

_____

_____

4. You and Your Roles
a) Where, if anywhere, in your life do you play the role of Scientist?

_____

_____

b) Who or what do you observe?

_____

_____

5. Do you play any of the following roles − in the literal or broad sense − in any part of your life? If not, would you like to? What might be your first step towards doing so?

Reformer   Inventor   Humanitarian
Revolutionary   Truth Seeker   Systems Analyst

_____

_____

6. Sun Aspects
If any of the following planets aspects your Sun, add each of the keywords for that planet to complete the following sentences. Which phrases ring true for you?

I am _____

My father is _____

My job requires that I am _____

Saturn Words (Use only if your Sun is aspected by Saturn)

ambitious	controlling	judgmental	mature
serious	strict	traditional	bureaucratic
cautious	committed	hard-working	disciplined
depressive	responsible	status-seeking	limiting

Uranus Words (Use only if your Sun is aspected by Uranus)

freedom-loving	progressive	rebellious	shocking
scientific	cutting-edge	detached	contrary
friendly	disruptive	eccentric	humanitarian
innovative	nonconformist	unconventional	exciting

Neptune Words (Use only if your Sun is aspected by Neptune)

sensitive	idealistic	artistic	impressionable
disappointing	impractical	escapist	self-sacrificing
spiritual	unrealistic	dreamy	glamorous
dependent	deceptive	rescuing	blissful

Pluto Words (Use only if your Sun is aspected by Pluto)

powerful	single-minded	intense	extreme
secretive	rotten	passionate	mysterious
investigative	uncompromising	ruthless	wealthy
abusive	regenerative	associated with sex, birth or death	

a) If one or more negative words describe you or your job, how might you turn that quality into something more positive or satisfying?

_____

_____

7. The Moon and You

Below are brief lists of what the Moon needs, in the various elements, to feel secure and satisfied. First find your Moon element, then estimate how much of each of the following you are expressing and receiving in your life, especially at home and in your relationships, on a scale of 0 to 5 where 0 = none and 5 = plenty.

FIRE MOONS — Aries, Leo, Sagittarius

attention	action	drama
recognition	self-expression	spontaneity
enthusiasm	adventure	leadership

EARTH MOONS — Taurus, Virgo, Capricorn

stability	orderly routine	sensual pleasures
material security	a sense of rootedness	control over your home life
regular body care	practical achievements	pleasurable practical tasks

AIR MOONS — Gemini, Libra, Aquarius

mental rapport	stimulating ideas	emotional space
friendship	social justice	interesting conversations
fairness	socialising	freedom to circulate

WATER MOONS — Cancer, Scorpio, Pisces

intimacy	a sense of belonging	emotional rapport
emotional safety	respect for your feelings	time and space to retreat
acceptance	cherishing and being cherished	warmth and comfort

a) Do you feel your Moon is being 'fed' enough?

yes _____ no _____

b) How might you satisfy your Moon needs even better?

_____

_____

8. You and Your Mercury

As an Aquarian, your Mercury can only be in Capricorn, Aquarius or Pisces. Below are some of the ways and situations in which Mercury in each of the elements might learn and communicate effectively. First find your Mercury sign, then circle the words you think apply to you.

Mercury in Fire (As an Aquarian, you can never have Mercury in a fire sign; the words are included here for completeness)

action   imagination   identifying with the subject matter
excitement   drama   playing with possibilities

Mercury in Earth (Capricorn)

time-tested methods   useful facts   well-structured
                                                          information
'how to' instructions   demonstrations   hands-on experience

Mercury in Air (Aquarius)

facts arranged in   logic   demonstrable connections
categories
rational arguments   theories   debate and sharing of ideas

Mercury in Water (Pisces)

pictures and images   charged atmospheres   feeling-linked
                                                                            information
intuitive understanding emotional rapport   being shown
                                                                            personally

a) This game with Mercury can be done with a friend or on your own. Skim through a magazine until you find a picture that interests you. Then describe the picture – to your friend, or in writing or on tape. Notice what you emphasise and the kind of words you use. Now try to describe it using the language and emphasis of each of the other Mercury modes. How easy did you find that? Identifying the preferred Mercury style of others and using that style yourself can lead to improved communication all round.

9. Your Venus Values
Below are lists of qualities and situations that your Venus sign

might enjoy. Assess on a scale of 0 to 5 how much your Venus desires and pleasures are met and expressed in your life. 0 = not at all, 5 = fully.

Venus in Aries
You will activate your Venus by taking part in anything that makes you feel potent, for example:

taking the initiative	competition	risk-taking
action dramas	taking the lead	tough challenges

Venus in Sagittarius
You will activate your Venus through following your adventurous spirit, opening up new frontiers and sharing your enthusiasm with others, for example:

travelling	sport	searching for the meaning of life
teaching or preaching	inspiring others	publishing or broadcasting

Venus in Capricorn
You will activate your Venus through anything that makes you feel a respected member of the community, for example:

doing your duty	upholding tradition	working towards goals
achieving ambitions	heading a dynasty	acquiring social status

Venus in Aquarius
You will activate your Venus through freedom from the restraints of convention, for example:

sharing progressive ideas	unusual relationships	being nonconformist
humanitarian projects	teamwork	eccentric fashions

Venus in Pisces
You will activate your Venus through anything that allows you to experience fusion with something greater than yourself, for

example:

| relieving suffering | daydreaming | creating a glamorous image |
| spiritual devotion | voluntary service | losing yourself in art, music or love |

a) How, and where, might you have more fun and pleasure by bringing more of what your Venus sign loves into your life?

_____

_____

b) Make a note here of the kind of gifts your Venus sign would love to receive. Then go on and spoil yourself . . .

_____

_____

Resources

Finding an Astrologer

I'm often asked what is the best way to find a reputable astrologer. Personal recommendation by someone whose judgement you trust is by far the best way. Ideally, the astrologer should also be endorsed by a reputable organisation whose members adhere to a strict code of ethics, which guarantees confidentiality and professional conduct.

Contact Addresses

Association of Professional Astrologers
www.professionalastrologers.org

APA members adhere to a strict code of professional ethics.

Astrological Association of Great Britain
www.astrologicalassociation.co.uk

The main body for astrology in the UK that also has information on astrological events and organisations throughout the world.

Faculty of Astrological Studies
www.astrology.org.uk

The teaching body internationally recognised for excellence in astrological education at all levels.

Your Aquarian Friends

You can keep a record of Aquarians you know here, with the page numbers of where to find their descriptions handy for future reference.

Name _____ Date of Birth _____

Aspects*	None	Saturn	Uranus	Neptune	Pluto

Moon Sign _____ p _____
Mercury Sign _____ p _____
Venus Sign _____ p _____

Name _____ Date of Birth _____

Aspects*	None	Saturn	Uranus	Neptune	Pluto

Moon Sign _____ p _____
Mercury Sign _____ p _____
Venus Sign _____ p _____

Name _____ Date of Birth _____

Aspects*	None	Saturn	Uranus	Neptune	Pluto

Moon Sign _____ p _____
Mercury Sign _____ p _____
Venus Sign _____ p _____

Name _____ Date of Birth _____

Aspects*	None	Saturn	Uranus	Neptune	Pluto

Moon Sign _____ p _____
Mercury Sign _____ p _____
Venus Sign _____ p _____

* Circle where applicable

Sign Summaries

SIGN	GLYPH	APPROX DATES	SYMBOL	ROLE	ELEMENT	QUALITY	PLANET	GLYPH	KEYWORD
1. Aries	♈	21/3–19/4	Ram	Hero	Fire	Cardinal	Mars	♂	Assertiveness
2. Taurus	♉	20/4–20/5	Bull	Steward	Earth	Fixed	Venus	♀	Stability
3. Gemini	♊	21/5–21/6	Twins	Go-Between	Air	Mutable	Mercury	☿	Communication
4. Cancer	♋	22/6–22/7	Crab	Caretaker	Water	Cardinal	Moon	☽	Nurture
5. Leo	♌	23/7–22/8	Lion	Performer	Fire	Fixed	Sun	☉	Glory
6. Virgo	♍	23/8–22/9	Maiden	Craftworker	Earth	Mutable	Mercury	☿	Skill
7. Libra	♎	23/9–22/10	Scales	Architect	Air	Cardinal	Venus	♀	Balance
8. Scorpio	♏	23/10–23/11	Scorpion	Survivor	Water	Fixed	Pluto	♇	Transformation
9. Sagittarius	♐	22/11–21/12	Archer	Adventurer	Fire	Mutable	Jupiter	♃	Wisdom
10. Capricorn	♑	22/12–19/1	Goat	Manager	Earth	Cardinal	Saturn	♄	Responsibility
11. Aquarius	♒	20/1–19/2	Waterbearer	Scientist	Air	Fixed	Uranus	♅	Progress
12. Pisces	♓	20/2–20/3	Fishes	Dreamer	Water	Mutable	Neptune	♆	Universality